FULL MOON

FULL MOON

An Anthology of
Canadian Women Poets

Quadrant Editions 1983

Published with the kind assistance of the Ontario Arts Council and the Canada Council.

Quadrant Editions
R.R. #1, Dunvegan
Ontario

Quadrant Editions are distributed in Canada by:
Volume Incorporated
3636 boul. St. Laurent
Montreal, Quebec

And in the United States by:
Flat Iron Distribution
Dover Book Distribution Centre
51 Washington Street
Dover, New Hampshire
U.S.A.   03820

Typeset in Baskerville by Resistance Typographers, Edmonton, and printed by Hignell, Winnipeg.

Canadian Cataloguing in Publication Data
Main entry under title:

Full moon

Poems
ISBN 0-86495-028-4

1. Canadian poetry (English) — Women authors.*
2. Canadian poetry (English) — 20th century.*
I. LaDuke, Janice II. Luxton, Steve, 1948-

PS8283.W6F84 1983 C811'.54'0809287 C84-090025-2
PR9195.3.F84 1983

For my mother
S.L.

For Josie
J.L.

TABLE OF CONTENTS

TABLE OF CONTENTS

TABLE OF CONTENTS

TABLE OF CONTENTS

my bands of silk and miniver
Momentarily grew heavier;
The black gauze was beggarly thin;
The ermine muffled mouth and chin;
I could not suck the moonlight in.

— Elinor Wylie
from ''Full Moon''

No. Not for her
no tears
I held the moon in my belly
nine months duration
then she burst forth
an outcry of poems.

— Dorothy Livesay
''Ballad of Me''

The moon and its rhythms have long served as symbols for women. They stand for what the new woman deeply knows: only in free and independent movement can fullness and creativity be achieved. The lunar face illuminates more than one poem found here.

The purpose of this collection of poetry by women is therefore two-fold. First, it is to help in the unfinished task of communicating woman's freed consciousness. Second, because this compilation is a literary and artistic one, it is to provide exposure to a number of very accomplished Canadian poets who are also women.

Much has been written of late concerning the treatment that history has afforded to the poetry of women. Their work has had to struggle hard against the biases of what Jacques Derrida terms a "phallocentric" culture and society. Nineteenth century males coined the term "Treacle Verse" to dismiss the poetic efforts of the "fairer sex". Because it steered clear of the male infatuation with combat and heroics, women's verse was denounced as garrulous, illogical and sentimental. Stressing the humane and personal values, it nevertheless earned a huge 'female' readership. This popularity was another attribute that confirmed the prejudice of the male critical establishment.

No warmer reception, however, greeted the female writers who did write in modes other than sentimental and "popular". Writing frankly of the primary concerns of their sex, their behaviour was deemed scandalous. By showing such integrity, these artists gave up all hope of publication, or had to "defeminize" themselves. The list of serious nineteenth century poets who adopted masculine names is long.

Patriarchal values prevail in our own century. Consequently, the male critical establishment rewards the mode of poetry most congenial to it. This, feminist critics assert, is a sculpted verse featuring wit and ideas rather than feeling, and an engagement with the outer world rather than the inner. For the sake of convenience we might term this, goal-oriented poetry.

Its opposite number is a poetry which is more open than closed in form, more confessional than externalized, and more in tune with feelings than ideas.

It is this inclusive mode that seems to be preferred by Twentieth Century women. A look at the poems in *Full Moon* confirms this. At the same time, it reveals that the application of ideologically derived categories does only so much justice...

On these pages confessionalist, self-disclosing poems abound. We have Elizabeth Allen's heart-rending poem of isolation and loss ("Preparing for Winter"), Mary di Michele's and Carolyn Smart's vulnerable celebrations of female friendship ("The Passion Artists" and "Flying"), and Bronwen Wallace's revelation concerning helplessness ("Dreams of Rescue"). With few exceptions — Bronwen Wallace's and Sharon Nelson's quasi-narrative pieces — the poems are lyrics often sharing an affirmative if rather sad, meditative mood. Most of them are also engaged in an open-handed manner with the inward world. There are poems about isolation (Allen), the confusion and perplexities of identity (Brewster, Cadsby, MacPhee, Keating, Nelson), domestic oppression and maintenance (Nelson, Sarah, Welch), conflicts involved with the bearing and keeping of children (Brown, Davis, Jones), women relating to women (di Michele, Smart, Wallace) and women relating to others (Allen, Kogawa, Wallace). Also featured are poems of witchcraft, magic and incantation — those more traditional roads to power for women (Hayes, Keating).

Thus far, the generalizations hold true.

Other poems, however, don't fit our analytical categories. Open form, the other mode congenial to women writers, is rarer here (Diana Haye's "Take Your Heart to the River" and Paddy Webb's glistening poem "grandmother"). The closed form, has been harshly criticized as patriarchal, though it hardly seems so in the hands of Diane Keating, Susan Glickman and Maggie Helwig. Moreover, the work of Glickman and especially of Helwig could be classified not only as sculpted but non-confessional. Yet the expression of sympathy and compassion in Helwig's "The Cripples" and "The Numbering at Bethlehem" is far from stultified. Are we to dismiss her poem, "The Pink Blouse", which celebrates transcendence, simply as absorbed with an irrelevant masculine concern? And what exactly are we to do with "language" poetry? *Full Moon* amply reveals that rich language can serve the emotive and processive style as well as the taut and objective.

Truth lies in the recognition that generalizations are not definities. Helpful as the former are, they should be tempered by other considerations. The sensibility and achievement of an accomplished poet is energized by many factors: her sex, her culture, her temperament, her class , her region, and more. The poems published here were selected not only for their pertinence but for their individual power, fullness, and quality. We hope you, female or male, are similarly moved.

Janice LaDuke and Steve Luxton
Ayer's Cliff and Montreal, Quebec
November, 1983

————————— *ELIZABETH ALLEN* —————————

Elizabeth Allen was born in New Zealand, and came to Canada in 1975. She lives in south-eastern Saskatchewan on a farm. She began writing seriously in 1976 after attending a creative writing workshop at the Saskatchewan Summer School of the Arts. Her first book of poetry, "A Shored Up House", published by Turnstone Press, won the Gerald Lampert Memorial Award from the League of Canadian Poets and Writers' Union. She is now working on a new manuscript of poetry, "Territories".

SEASONS

the ritual begins
the lace of snowmould
lingers
on dampened grass

again she takes on the season
bends in her garden
planting rows of beans & carrots

watches two deer in the pasture
something she'd like to share
like the days
when she wants
to bake bread
fill the house
with its smell of welcome

but summer is not always warm
sometimes there are berries
sometimes the branches are barren

each year so different
however hard she tries
to compare them

when crows
thread blackness across the sky
she stands inside the house
where she stored her summer
feels a sadness
she doesn't understand

PREPARING FOR WINTER

if you had held your hand out to me
just once in the last long season,
i wouldn't have minded so much
the wind buffeting the house from all sides,
the gaunt trees swaying thin branches
to its erratic music.

but for us there was no meeting
of eyes at the hearth
when snow came to blanket the land.
you were locked, as the trees are
locked into the season.

now in bluffs that shelter the sloughs
with their summer-green swatch of leaves,
i pick wild rose petals in my basket,
make fragrant preserves.

in fall when the sloughs are dry,
ringed with empty snail shells, and dead
leaves skitter over cracked earth
to tangle in the warp of willow branches,
i go picking the red splash of rosehips
to colour my solitary winters with tea.

BRUISES

when i ask you
why you do not love me anymore
you say
today you were going to bring me pussywillows
but were distracted
by seven white-tailed deer
startled from the bush
you had stopped at

yesterday it was crocuses
forgotten on the hillside
among the ones you didn't pick
purple heads swaying
in thin & brittle grass
their petals soft as skin

HOMESTEAD

the crippled deer
crossing the lane on a frosty morning
is of the land
as you are   now

you begin to know
where berry bushes are
more plentiful
where coyotes
sing down the moon

& in spring
when geese draw the sun
up from the south
you begin again
to store images of summer
a cellarful to keep you warm
when they pull the sun south again
drawing down the winter night

──────────────── *ROO BORSON* ────────────────

Roo Borson's book of poetry, "A Sad Device", was published by Quadrant Editions in 1982. Her book "Rain", from which the following poems were extracted, was published by Penumbra Press.

RAIN

The plunging, lumbering sea
four of us walking
the North Shore lucid
          with emeralds
            clean
the lighthouse sweeping the water
with its thin arm of an angel
sometimes
everything we are in the city of men drifts off
it will come back to us
sleep will set things in order
the way
            fog burns off the hills
                traceless
          but really wandering
            high over cities
        that burn like handfuls of gold
the way a forest burns
all the way down
the way
one lives
high over the harbour
in a house looking down
and wave-caught stones
           running at the shore
             smash up
        the way
dinner is prepared
over and again
the laden plates
and the children growing
mercilessly
out from under you
        the bananas lie in their bowl
        and smile sideways the way
your mind is going
lousing it up
again

your husband's innocence so
violent his hands come at you
like pages
you would turn them
over
ah spring
brings its revival
of restlessness

how you cannot live
all your life in this house
elsewhere made whole by him
who tears you in half
who throws you away and won't tell you
you're thrown away

the firs stand tall
in their hairsuit of needles
the hemlock
fills with bloodlight
another day gone down

and the hollow plink of pebbles
and the sky drifting east
endlessly
the large crowd
of men
drifting forward
through time
that has
no backward
the way a man
makes one pass only
at what he loves
and misses

we four are walking
the driftwood smells of lilac and smoke
the dead fish
silvery

at our feet
amulets
the gulls
making bracelets
around the night
the foam's anklets
clasp us
even now the dead slaves washing ashore from
Africa
what
larger purpose
has done to us
that it is not
purpose but
an accidental collision
like that of
two jets holding five hundred each
unwieldly like golden civilizations grown too large
colliding
and all the people
tumbling out
it is impossible
that a life is made up of days
my whole life
is like making a name for myself
in a foreign country
because the nights
are a tangle of black wind
black leaves and love
and why two animals
say hello
before they make love
it is how
the calf comes out of the wrong end of a cow
how they are one creature
at birthing
two-headed
or a box which contains
an infinity of smaller boxes
Jane
I say this to you

we four were walking
and nothing touched except our insides

sometimes all of this is ours
to make of what we will
we can lie back in the arms of men
in our own minds
and hold back awhile
hold back the speech
inevitably misunderstood
           the way a woman
              might make only one try
            for the man she loves first
               and miss
Jane, it is that way

and your husband's innocence lies under
           everything you touch
              including
the other one
      whose disparagement of innocence is
            his innocence
        don't let him surprise you
      who tries to know what he does

in the last century
there always came a time
to return home after
the long trek
the long war
but this is the century in which
we have to walk barefoot past all that
the century we have so far to go
maybe we won't make it back
this time

10

Dark ankles slide
down the white sand path
of thimbleberry
salmonberry
down toward the sea
on which floats a log
on which there are three birds
black silouette
on the moving ground
of ocean
three dark birds riding a log
for a few minutes
in the universe

this time I want to tell you these things
not because you need to hear them
but because
they just come out this way
there is such a thing as
talking
these three birds know this

the thimbleberries
tangle in the air
they grow up out of the sand
with sand on their leaves
all things being joined to their landscapes

it is not sad what becomes of 2 people
it is almost enough to say that we
smile against each other in the dark
a little while
but there is more

that clouds are blown in
& break in half
releasing rain
and then move on

that for a moment
three dark birds
sharing a dark log
ride the ocean

20

Phosphorescent lace
black glass waves
lights
on the harbour
jostling
you walk along
the grass a dim crushed
perfume
delicate as black spines of shrimp

the perfect pink shrimp
like lanterns
deep in the ocean

carrying that thin black wire
that has only to quiver
to go out

and the lights also
the whole North Shore

the seahorses
their small skeletons
knobby
curling & unfurling their tails
their leglessness
their eyes like tiny ships
seeing everything
in all directions
from birth to death
the seahorses
charging in slow motion
fanning out
deep deep in the live black ocean
stepping barefoot
down gelatinous sand at waterline
the cold ache shooting up your legs
walking all the way to the point

to the planetarium
with its great metal crab
the raised pincers shining
stars
reflectionless in the deep ruffled harbour
alive with oysters
pumping their water & refuse
in & out
like hearts
and the stars as if at anchor
just above the harbour
actually
they are nowhere near

and the North Shore glitters
you close your eyes
to keep the light inside
forever
like someone living only once
who passes what he sees
through him
to others
like a thing whispered
around a room for a game
the thing whispered
is the same story
changing hands
history
half-clamshells shut on the sand
like the eyelids of sleepers
the lights the people

and walking back —
to what? —
past the sign informing
there will be no ball-playing
or nudity on the beach
under the blue fluorescent lights
clotted with moths
past the half-illumined masks of flowers

past the corner grocery with its packages
its cans gleaming
in the wayward streetlight
the huge faces
of apartment buildings
painted colors no one would choose
for themselves

you lie in bed
figuring things out
figuring
there's no way out in particular
being alive
here now & never again

knowing
you will live & leave no mark

hearing
over & over in the distance
the waves'

broken jaws
close on nothing

starlight
through the open window
silent
like rain

ELIZABETH BREWSTER

Elizabeth Brewster was born in Chipman, New Brunswick. She has studied and taught at various universities and now lives in Saskatoon where she teaches at the University of Saskatchewan. An accomplished writer, she has published nine volumes of poetry, two novels, and one volume of short stories.

DOUBLE INVENTORY

A few score of poems
a score of short stories
two novels
a bundle of diaries
scribblers full of dreams
some lecture notes
and committee minutes:

that's the total my life amounts to

(some students, maybe,
whose names I don't remember)

Can I place this up against
my friend's four children,
her solid husband,
her small-town house full of
inherited clocks
and home-stitched quilts,
her country cottage
with its kitchen garden
and its oatfield sloping
down to the bay?

See how she has tended
vegetables and children,
freed them from weeds,
made them grow
tall and healthy,
her hands brown
with the soil of their growth,
her heavy brogues squelching in
mulch and humus

And count all the breakfasts
she has placed before them,
the cakes she has baked,
the number of times

she has polished the chairs
with furniture polish
and waxed the kitchen floor
...committee minutes:

the games of scrabble in the evenings,
dominoes, card games,
books read aloud as a child went to sleep

the shoes and faces shined
for Sunday church

Now they are all grown up,
all schooled, all working,
two of the boys married.

We sit together at her kitchen table,
eat the tomatoes and lettuce
she grew in her garden

envy one another.

Back in high schol
we took turns leading our classes,
finished with a tie
for second place

Still equals
we have managed
passably
to make something grow

DISPLACED PERSON

She was born in Russia, spent her youth in France,
now, at fifty,
lives in a basement apartment in a small town
in the American mid-West.
She has four cats
which take turns sitting on her shoulder
when she drinks a glass of hot tea.
"They have more courtesy," she says,
"than most of the people."

Her walls are covered
with maps instead of windows,
Russia or Greece or Egypt.
She wants to go to Mexico for the heat
and to Montreal
for the sake of the beautiful cold.

Meanwhile, sometimes she spends
a week-end in Chicago
or an evening watching a foreign movie,
or cooks exotic dinners
which the cats, having been born in Wisconsin
and brought up on milk and cat food,
do not always like.

ASSIGNMENT

I have asked my freshmen
to hand in diaries
forget to write my own.

The same alarm clock
wakes them all up in the morning.
They queue for books
listen to professors
who are, or are not, funny.

But there are differences:

some have children
or rhubarb in the back yard
are concerned about bank loans
or baby-sitters
while others spend all night at parties
get tickets for speeding through small towns
and think life is Wow.

I write notes in the margins.
Is this essay exceptional,
very good, good, or merely adequate?

Shouldn't this girl buy a dictionary,
look up the use of the apostrophe,
avoid dangling modifiers,
write "I went to bed" instead of "I retired"?

I take a rest from the assignment

dig potatoes and beets in my own back garden
black soil under my finger-nails
bring in the last of the tomatoes
before they are touched by frost,
put them in paper bags to ripen.

At the front of the house the hedge needs clipping
where it's tangled itself around the gate.
There are leaves on the lawn to be raked
though why bother
when the wind will blow more over
from the neighbours' trees?

"Don't be so allegorical"
I say to the falling leaves
as they land in my hair.
"You try too hard."

Garbage, are they, or compost?

RONNIE R. BROWN

Ronnie R. Brown was born and raised in Massachusetts. She studied at the University of Massachusetts in Amherst and at Montreal's Concordia University where she completed a B.A. and M.A. (in creative writing) and was the recipient of both the Board of Governor's Award for poetry (1975-76) and the Festival of The Arts Graduate Award (1980). She presently lives in Ottawa where she works in broadcasting and teaches part-time at both Concordia University and at Carleton University. Her work has appeared in "Los", "Rune", "Arc", "Montreal Writers' Forum", "Event", and "Cross Canada Writers' Quaterly". She is one of the eleven new poets spotlighted in Quadarnt Editions recent anthology, "The Inner Ear".

FINGERS AND TOES
for Philip

Before the light
can fight its way
past the protective
shades, the whisper comes.
"Today?" my son asks huskily
his eyes still slit with sleep.
My "yes" awakens the world
(at least in our vicinity).
Shades and lids snap open
to his high-pitched "Hooray!"

"Five years old *today*,"
he recites this solemnly,
as he holds up the four
small fingers which for
the year have helped him
to depict, graphically,
the measure of his maturity.
Then slowly from where he's palmed it
a well-sucked thumb takes its rightful place.
Wonder pools on his face, spreads gradually
to smile, as he declares
awe-fully, "I'm a *whole hand* now!"

And I, who saw his tiny head
still slick with birth cupped
in his father's hand, am awe
struck too.
First comes one hand, then two —
at ten a handful of another variety.
Next, one by one, feet will join in
the count. Each step
moving him
from me.

I hold out my hands to him,
he holds on willingly and for
the briefest moment we
stand silently
bridging the inevitable
divide.

NIGHTFEEDING

Your cry
sends me
plunging in-
to action. Half-
asleep, guided by
sonar, I
seek you out.
Little amphibian,
you flail,
drowning in air until
you sense my milky
presence there:
float,
safely secured
in an ark
of arms,
sucking me in.

HEATHER CADSBY

Heather Cadsby was born in Belleville, Ontario, and has lived in Canada all her life. She did her university studies at McMaster. She is married and has two children. Her poetry has appeared in "Quarry", "Canadian Forum", "Prism', "Malahat Review", "CVII", and "The Dalhousie Review". Her first book of poems, "Traditions", was published by Fiddlehead Poetry Books in 1982.

14 IS STILL MINE

At noon she shuffles to the porch
in her father's old bathrobe,
holds her hair and takes in the day.
She stands my height, wearing my love's clothes.
I say she is clearly ours
and yet her soft body is growing removed.
I want to hold her, rock her in my arms,
love her fiercely.
I want her in our bed forever.
I want to rest my eyes on her beauty.
But look
she's off in a flash
of water some summer boy threw on her head
as she grabbed his ankle,
sent him flapping on the sand.
This too is love.
This forgotten moment
that let's her survive a mother's grip.

WHAT THEY NEVER TELL YOU

Egyptian women rolled papyrus leaves.
Romans preferred soft wool.
Africans made do with grass.
Others took to their beds.

French nurses in the Great War
found surgical bandages handy.
After the war a bright Frenchman
hit the jackpot
selling surplus bandage material
calling it Kotex.

One day I learned to walk
straddling a colossus.
My mother said
thank goodness.
My father, being Welsh,
burst into song.

Some day my little daughter
will ask.

GREEN AGAIN

My sister is colossal.
She's so big
she's my mother's only topic.
The smile on her moon face
is fixed on smug hands
spread conspicuously
on her pumpkin belly.
Each plump finger says,
I own all of this.
The message is ten-fold.
How she loves her richness.
How secret it is.
And I who fight to stay thin
want whatever it is she's got.
I dream of
bags of gold under my coat
a cache of jewels pinned to my slip
crates of caviar in the folds of my dress.
It must be grand
to love yourself that big
to say proudly to clerks,
This doesn't fit. Bring me something larger.
My sister encloses
the biggest mystery in the world
and the secret is
that I who want no more children
want my sister's baby.

ANOREXIA NERVOSA

These skin and bones won't eat.
There's nothing to love.
They're rid of most of themselves.
Now they're going for broke.

Forced tubes won't fatten them up.
They think you're a witch
and charm you with moony beauty
they've grown through starving.
These waifs will do anything
to preserve it.

Rounded out they'd be regular,
and they must be special.
Bony things like that are attended to.
They've topped their destroyers.
They are their own worms.

LORNA CROZIER

Lorna Crozier was born in 1948 in Swift Current, Saskatchewan. She has published four books of poetry under the name of Lorna Uher: "Inside Is the Sky", "Crow's Black Joy", "No Longer Two People" (co-authored with Patrick Lane), and "Humans and Other Beasts". This fall a fifth collection, "The Weather", will be published by Coteau Books. Lorna has taught for several years at the Saskatchewan Summer School of Arts. This year as the recipient of an arts' award, she is writing full-time.

STILLBORN

who
looped the cord
around his fine new neck

who
hanged him
in my bone gallows my

beautiful son
blue as the blue
in Chinese porcelain

WOMAN FROM THE WEST COAST

The beautiful one, the woman
who wears long flowered skirts
that cling to her legs
as if the wind were water
tells me that what I call sage
is not.
     It's witch's moss
                she says
    I grow it in my garden
    have for years.

She is an expert. She's read
all the names in books
and uses herbs to make
her spells. In an almanac
she records shapes of the moon
times of tides and planting.

I have lived on the prairie
all my life   have rubbed
the silver-green of sage
into my skin   crushed the leaves
in my hair   laid them
on the eyelids of my lover.
I wonder what
she'll call the wind.

WILD GEESE

The wild geese fly
the same pathways
they have followed for centuries.

There is comfort in this
though they are not the same
geese my mother listened to
when she was young.

Perhaps I first heard them
inside of her
as she watched their wings
eclipse the moon, their call
the first sound — separate
from the soft, aquatic
whispers of the womb.

And my sadness is her sadness
passed through generations
like distance and direction
and the longing
for the nesting ground.

PAVLOVA

Even you, Pavlova, you
with the beautiful feet and arms
even you did not die
with grace or beauty.
Your last words
Get my swan costume ready
were what we would have written
for you, but death would not
lift you weightless
into the bright air.

You waited
in the shadow of the wings,
moistening your lips,
crossing yourself as you had
a hundred times before.
Should I have had children instead?
Sons and daughters
to show pictures to.
This is the country I left,
see why I weep.

In Russia the snow is falling
as it does in memory, falling
from the backs of horses
settling in the furs of women
who ride to the concert halls.
In your garden in England
the swan who laid his neck
across your shoulders
and bit your flesh
in his dark unpredictable beak
dreams himself whole again
up to where the sky
was made for swans.

Lonely and sick you lie
in a Dutch hotel.
Your lungs like stones
press you into the bed.
Clutching your husband's hand,
you feel the warmth of the mistress
he left just moments ago,
hear his words
She will not dance tomorrow,
as the doctor cuts
into your ribcage
to drain the pus
and let the breath in.

──────────── *FRAN DAVIS* ────────────

Fran Davis is a teacher of literature and writing at Vanier College in Montreal. She gives public lectures, writing workshops and poetry readings both in Montreal and elsewhere. She has published poetry, fiction and book reviews in such publications as "Canadian Forum", "Canadian Woman Studies", "CVII", "Dalhousie Review", "Cross/Cut", "Fiddlehead", "Montreal Poetry", "Montreal Sampler", "Quarry", "Saturday Night at the Forum", "There is a Voice", and "Versus". Her first published mystery story will appear in "Prime Crimes II, an anthology of mystery writing to be published in December, 1984.

READING YOUR BONES

I used to watch your heartbeat through the fontanel.
After the bones closed, I went on imagining it,
the bright pulse of the blood I gave you
beating beneath pale oat-coloured hair.
You grew, and finally I could not even find the place,
your skull so rounded, separate, alone.

When I take you now to the barber
and he begins to cut away the thatch above your eyes
baring the flower stalk of neck
the naked question mark of ears
I find myself watching again, expectant:

Will you open your secrets to me?
Is some of my blood still beating there?

TO MY SON

drifting upon the deep
dream of your beginnings
the flux of your flesh
rounded itself and the skull
bones formed a globe
tunnelled through airless dark
and then burst free

all wet and serpentine
your hair, slicked to the scalp
darkly defined your orbit
till widening, your world
went ringed like Saturn
circles of golden need
ecstatically circling me

eyes first mirrors
of the immense not-you
became more opaque and wore
their secrets in a gray-green sea
hair thickened like willow bark
roughening brownly round the bole
declaring you definitely

new continents of feature formed
each day; now from the angle
of your jaw come tremors
of fierce deliberation
orbits erratic, eager
equations of your own
concentric male geometry

———————— *MARY di MICHELE* ————————

*Mary di Michele is a poet and editor whose fourth collection of poems:
"Necessary Sugar" is forthcoming from Oberon press in 1984. Her work
has appeared in anthologies, including Atwood's "Oxford Book of Cana-
dian Verse" and many magazines and literary periodicals including "Cana-
dian Forum", "Exile", "Tamarack Review", "Toronto Life",
"Canadian Literature", "Poetry Australia"...etc. She is one of the four
subjects of a film about poetry and poets, tentatively called AS FOR US,
directed by Bronwen Wallace and Chris Whynot.*

THE PASSION ARTISTS
for Carolyn Smart

On the table, a pot of white chrysanthemums,
glass conducting the duet of female voices
to ice tinkling in aperitifs.

You begin again to tell me the part,
to try to give me a clue
that will help me to divine
the past, accept every property
of the new chemical I've become
because of my latest catalyst, a man.
You are always lured back to your drink
to the lighted end of a cigarette,
thirty years of talking too much
slackening the flesh around your jaw.

Sometimes we can't imagine a future
except as the present amplified
turning up the volume of the stereo,
playing "Diamonds and Rust",
a lousy poet with something to say
and no will to imagine anything better
than her love affair with the sixties.

Our summer evening, sleeveless and smoking,
a batik of ultramarine and pink,
displayed for us from your balcony.
Pigeons coo, dance along the rail,
grey birds wearing their feathers
like feminists in faded denim,
a bandana of mother of pearl
around their necks.
The whirr of those wings
making me pregnant
with a desire for flight.
I nurse the thought whenever I'm fucked up
with the love of a dozen men or one man
I wanted to ride out the future with.

From the window, we have an idea of sky
and other apartments to the north,
a few lights aroused for tired men,
home from work, for whom even stars
have to be accounted for and taxed.
Here I want to believe in cities
built for people to live together,
but every door on this floor
including ours is locked,
like arteries choking in nuggets of fat,
insurance against feeling forever.

We talk all night about great literature and men,
Simone de Beauvoir, vow to drink
tea with her in Paris.
"I'd leave him", you say,
"if I could find a man I liked
better."

Shrill cries of a siren penetrate the sanctum,
we open a bottle of rhine wine
pour it into frosted glasses.
There is a flashing light at the back of my mind
a sure knowledge that I am only dangerous
to myself.

Mascara punctuates the corners of your eyes
concealing the look you save
for your moments alone with the mirror,
a prim beauty worn with discomfort,
pewter tinted lace at neck and wrists,
sold by old crones at Simpson's
whose undergarments are stored
with sachets of pot pourri,
proof that a woman respects herself.

We can't even make a dirty joke of it!
The passion we imagine, too rarefied,
like the two headed beast Plato described
human beings to originally have been.

Our men's balls are wafers,
dry, holy, and without leavening,
we spread our tongues gingerly
to let them slip through
without being touched.

SINISTER CLOWNS

I

Darling, good night. Our city with its tiara lights
crowns my baby's sleep. Hand of love,
old hypnotist, can levitate her a foot
above the bed, a miracle like our lives
carrying on in spite of our worst
intentions.

Dropping its corners
her mouth rounds
into fish lips,
breathing bubbles of milk
from my breast,
eyes awash in that oriental dream,
an imagined or historical script:
in defense of walls, she has them
china blue eyes.

How to resist that narcotic
of beauty and poison in a man
when he slips on his fox gloves
with their clever purple thumbs:
a dilemma she inherits from me
and the tribe of women.

My daughter born into 1984
when the anti-passion leagues
have inherited a Double Dutch,
a game of sex,
a graffiti of sterile flesh
scrawled with the first skipping
of hormones, boys in the schoolyard
fistfuls of marbles
bulging their jeans.

II

I bed my better self first
then make my way
picking up toys to the study,
without her they stage a revolution,
animated by something other
than the clear stream of her mind,
sinister clowns questioning
what stuff preoccupies
my thoughts.

She sleeps in her room
hand clutching the air
where my body has been,
confident as in the instance
we sit in mid air
before a pratfall.

She won't rest without my warmth
at her fingertips,
even hurtling down the highway
she believes in my hand at the wheel.

I can't live without this child in my arms,
a palpable sunrise,
a spray of crimson gladiolas,
love blazing commitment
to life continuing on earth.

I leave her to move
through the rooms of our home
tethered to the larger hands
steering the planet

of men who govern the world
making toys and bombs,
their metaphysic learned from Marvel comics,
making believe they are
men of steel with unlimited powers,
so much they need to invent
their own form of kryptonite,
lose the earth in order to coin
a new kind of death.

The mathematics that gives us
access to the stars
is being used for a countdown
to zero
as if they were observing
all this from outer space
as if we were all
already gone.

WEARY OF LILACS

Lilacs in bloom in a breeze,
lavender arms in a ballet,
last spring they thundered
as massive clouds,
mauve precipitating perfume.

In the photograph my sister shot
of Emily and I in the garden,
my infant daughter's no bigger than my thumb.
The camera's perspective here
accounting for the gap
in truth
and that is how experience remembered
lies to us about our lives.

My hand is all that represents me
and seems to secure her
as a buttercup captures an elf
or lures a bee.

My daughter, no bigger than my thumb,
although it was a marriage,
not she who was premature,
she made me weary of the romance of lilacs,
the blonde man whose semen was scented
like buckwheat honey,
a sweetness mixed with urine.

I have a love that eats up all the lilacs
turns them around in her violet eyes,
makes them open with the auburn sun
reflected in her hair.

These are not Whitman's lilacs,
they bloomed last year.
Today they are breathless in the bud
as I write this poem
and that is how language lies about flowers,
making all lilacs, one lilac
and all such poems, literature.

A white cradle on the second story of a house
triumphs over Sullivan St.
wrenches all the green and heart shaped leaves
of the lilac bushes.

Although no birds sing
where every household harbours
two or three cats,
Emily trills like a robin,
my breast red with her crown.

---------------- *SUSAN GLICKMAN* ----------------

Susan Glickman was born in 1953 and grew up in Montreal. She studied, worked and travelled in Europe, Asia, and the U.S.A. before settling down to teach English at the University of Toronto. Her first book, "Complicity", was published in 1983 by Signal Editions of Vehicule Press.

FROM THE BALCONY

Andrea lies in a ten-year-old's sulk
in her backyard next door.
She always sprawls in the shade,
shutting out the ridiculous mirth of July.
I, au contraire, have no dignity,
and brown myself like a chicken.

I wonder what she's thinking.
I watch her pale knees shift against red gingham,
blockading her narrow chest.
She refuses to be consoled
by summer.

Guests at a garden party, the trees
whisper behind their hands.
The clouds are fleecy and fat
as poodles, the sky
disingenuous blue.

In Andrea's movie, this place
is not important. Trees, clouds, garden,
the lady next door with her notebook —
we're background, the scenery
that flows under the credits.
She's saving us up for a flashback
when her true story begins.

PASSING WORDS
for Dennis Lee

Nothing is easy, that's what we're all saying,
the bruised lovers finding a laugh at the back
of anguish, the baffled parents stuttering over how, how,
to say anything true
to the small ones whose nightmares are less frightening
than the world they wake to;
all of us numb over machines whose noise cannot crowd out
the problems we go home to.
Trying to keep things clear. Trying to keep headlines
out of kitchens, to keep cancer from soup and bread,
bombs out of the bedroom. These
only the big ones
the ones so big they can't be seen; fiery stars
obscured by daylight and the atmosphere of earth
that startle us when night draws back
its curtains.
Usually it's the ordinary problems that won't let go,
that heckle and jeer behind day's little triumphs —
failure of work, failure of play, failure
of love. But we all keep going, nothing
is easy we say, we say it
so easily.

THE PRICE OF STAMPS

Memory tucked under one arm
a shoebox full of letters
carried surreptitiously from place to place —
however many times I move, I can't
let go of it.

Letters from old lovers full of grinning evasions,
airmail blue transatlantic commandments,
parental warnings, witty postcards, notes from friends
bordered with Chinese flowers.

Sitting over a nescafe frappe,
cappucino, cafe con latte,
at the necessary corner
striped awning, red and green or blue and white
like the stamps I lick with a tongue
that has forgotten its own language,
I am always 18, with a new passport.
I still trust Michelin guides, and open my life
to strangers.

People don't write letters any more
but call stridently across cities
expecting a lit fire,
a waiting bottle of wine.
Too many phonecalls enter this room
shoulders first, beating down the door
without knocking.

People don't write letters any more.
I loose them like pigeons into the fraught city,
small fluencies, appeals
for an encounter.

GOING HOME
    for Roo Borson

Why does anyone ever go back to the place
she grew up in? For the way
the sun slants in the bedroom window
all those mornings
rising with coffee-smells and the voices of parents
discussing the news, radio summons to the world
you would one day be grown up in.

And their voices at night, in the next room.
Your father's murmur ebbing and flowing
your mother's high quick tones: a gull
circling the bay, looking for some place
to land.

Their voices were just there, like the ocean
a little too far off to swim in.
You still hear them in your head sometimes:
your name called across an empty street,
the smell of lemons drifting from a neighbour's garden
in February, in Toronto.

Driving across a continent after that
elusive odor,
you keep the radio on in case
you miss something. On the highway
you are nowhere, you are only in transit.
Everything you own is on wheels
and the telephone poles
wave you on;
the little towns you didn't know existed, so many,
measuring the miles between where you came from
and where you're going, home.

You want to see things very clearly.
The furrowed mud and bare trees,
primary colours of billboards and refrains of old songs,
the way they repeat themselves —
insisting that every place
is the same, wherever
the heart carries its baggage.

ORANGES

I

Sometimes you're walking down the street
and it's raining, say, and your collar's up; you shrink
inside your skin, see nothing, don't care to. And then
you stop for a red light and on the corner
an old woman bends over her bags with a look
of such radiance
you believe she has the answer to everything in there,
with the oranges and the carton of milk.
She is the mother
you lost before you were born; you wake out of your life
into your life, there by the mailbox, under the umbrellas.
She turns the corner, shuffling her feet, her stooped back
black as all the others; you lose her in the crowd,
you walk on. What were you thinking before,mathematics
of loss. The day
has been given you to start over, and you do.

II

On the road to Mycenae in the dog-days of June
    what glitter, what lanterns set in green
        abundance of orange-groves,
    heavy by roadside, untended,
        open to any hand.And passing
we gather some; mystery
    old as these walls, precious
        as Agamemnon's crown.

III

My grandfather could peel an orange
in one elaborate loop: a snake-skin shed
recoiled to mimic fruit.

My grandmother made roses out of radish
too dainty to eat, and tomato-crowns
edged in jagged red.

And when I serve my friends,
I too build garden, castle,
the land of heart's desire.

Enough
is as good as a feast. An orange,
the deepening wash of sunset, fields of poppies,
such perilous excess.

DIANA HAYES

Born in Toronto in 1955, Diana Hayes studied at the University of Victoria and U.B.C., receiving her B.A. and M.F.A. in Creative Writing. She worked as Poetry Editor for "Prism International" while at U.B.C. from '80-'82. Her poetry, articles and fiction have appeared in the following: "C.B.C. Anthology", "CVII", "Descant", "Event", "From An Island", "Island", "The Malahat Review", "Monday Magazine", "Poetry Canada Review" and many others. Her published works include "Two of Swords" (Co-editor with Garry McKevitt), "Moving Inland" (Fiddlehead Poetry Books) and "Choosing the Miracle" (forthcoming). For the past few years she has been living on Salt Spring Island and writing full time with the generous assistance of the Canada Council and a U.B.C. graduate fellowship. Her most recent work, from which "... The Moon's Work" is selected, has invited the voice of one Frederick Tibbs, pioneer of (the now charted) Arnet Island off Tofino, in a celebration to resurrect his once illustrious castle ' "Dreamisle".

TAKE YOUR HEART TO THE RIVER

When, in spring, she took her belly-grief
to the river's wide settlement, thick and spilling
with the season's wet harvest, that winged arc of whitewater
where piper willow clung to her hair and skin
as mateless pollen, then followed her to the bank's crest
There she spoke not in sentences
but small breaths that whispered
listen to the river

And in so many distant towns her man gone
with the coming of solstice, into the road's wide spaces
child in her not a fortnight discovered, and growing

Where mountains, The Cascades, towering Dutch Uncles
dressed for late frost, offered a wider perch
than any man's knees, bending to the river to swallow her whole

Down to the waterside in robes of healing sunlight
she stepped to the rapids, losing light to the river
while shadowed in broom and gorse, and the blue grouse drummed
a throaty memory

How she met with a chilly hug from the rippled water
wading quickly to her shins
How she knelt to it at once, with her feet
numb to the rapids' bite
How she persuaded her thighs
How she rested there, while the river drove an icy finger
to her womb

With the water's work she angled clean of the rock,
nestled a gypsy mat snug to the high water line,
fed her body to shore and lay under blushed sun

Three days passed, and two, finding her lithe and laired
edging to the riverside to drink and rinse her eyes
Soon her belly tightened, the new pain growing heavy
Soon she knelt to the river's voice, offering a gift
of small flesh, blood-vermilion, spilling to the currents
from between her broken knees

Not gravity or the moon mothered this wombless fish
in a pod of kissing rocks,
It sprung fins and the spotted scales of a trout,
eyes fern-hued and focused with its father's same craft
and soon edgy in a crowded pool, it breached the whitewater
cleared the currents and whistled downstream, full of the day's
tricks, and a precocious flip

And the woman free now in her river's dream to fashion the
child
knee-high to a polliwog, tells herself the water's a better teacher
can offer its heart a stronger lineage — (she'd follow
if her eyes were fins)
her man too far from the currents to dream at all.

AS SHADOWS THROUGH THESE HUNDRED TREES
for Angie

Waking predawn in the breast
of the islands, rouge meridian of sun
emerging from fire-globe through water,
eyes free of their forgotten circles,
minds rid of stubborn cause,
and the horses bridled in this near-light
where all wishes are spoken by the croak
of Raven high in Bongie's Wood,
telling us this is possible, yes
this is a place to mend limbs, wash
hands of their ache and gristle,
to make smooth again the feathers
of our waking dreams.

We were down the drive with the horses
to find our way to the island's jaw,
to the lake where everything rises
to greet us, Saint mary's water-hands alive,
knowing the movement of hooves
and our passing can free our muddled hearts,
these gentle inflections of light
the first moment of day.

We move smoothly,
our thighs rubbing soft sounds
to the horses' withers.
We knew we were riding in a time
of loss with all we had, a pack of grub
and tools for building shelter,
a blanket for autumn cover,
we were riding to the centre
of the island, to find the lake
a mirror and a door, a magnet drawing heat
where deer circle in the strong mirage of dawn

reflecting a full moon in their startled
dancing eyes, signalling the harvest.
Remembering the long pass in the years
before this was,
I watch my shadow ride to the madrones.
Can we move so freely into arms
as shadows through these hundred trees?

THIS IS THE MOON'S WORK

In this wide country time will stop
then start up at once. In a day
seasons change, the sky
always speaks of this.
All the passing in light,
then that startled black
with all manner of creatures crawling.

That we bar no danger
and no bright gifts from our hearts,
tell me this is so.
It is the moon's work that brings us here,
it will be the great flood to take us.

Moving to the far ends of the earth
as we do, trailing our bits of roots
like old potatoes gone to shoot,
planting that one piece of ourselves
for the crop to spread for harvest,
waiting for our families to rise up weeds
in this place we lay our feet upon.
A tuck of home.
To the reaches of the earth
to flee old lives, now to be taken
on the water's terms.

As the sea carves cradles in these cliffs,
so we are found on the lip
of an unhumored land, finding our imprint
in sand swept up in a day,
leaving no sure sign of foot or bone.
This is the place where each morning
we must walk the tideline
to negotiate our bodies.
At every ebb, the time
to take up new seed, to wash our eyes
of their careless reconstructions,
to hold in our hands a wing,
a stone, a celebration
at the void's small mercy.

And the lightkeepers
their eyes are prisms
refracting, multiplying, making music
of all this dark.
All their sleepless cries
for an instant realized,
every moment a difference in light,
another reaching incandescence.

Raw heart, poor hearts
we dwellers of inland and rock.
With no hands big enough
to hold such waterweight.
A tide of longing,
all the sorrows spoken
through water's language.
Everything tossed back then,
birthless.
All awash.

And looking to Lennard Light
are we such lazy pilgrims
to dance in the lee of the keeper's beacon?
To try from the cover of these cliffs
to hold such arrows of light
between impossible fingers?

Such things washed up
and recast. All weather
and danger drawn from the belly.
A fist of flesh in the shapes of stars
that do not hang from the sky.
All manner of creatures
building their scurry of tenements
to be taken by sea,
ransacked in the night
by the moon's work
until the stillness and the morning
allow the work of hands.

Busy scuttle of lives.
We too are navigated by these
seamless ties.
Come dawn, we will build up
what has been taken by night.

——————————————————*MAGGIE HELWIG*——————————————————

Maggie Helwig was born in 1961, and lives and writes in Peterborough, Ontario. Her first book, "Walking Through Fire", was published by Turnstone Press in 1981. Her poems have appeared in a variety of periodicals, and she is presently completing a novel set in Renaissance Florence.

CERTAIN NOTES FROM BRUEGEL

THE FALL OF THE REBEL ANGELS

I begin here. Suddenly shape
falls out on both sides of the flaming sword
and Michael on spider legs scrambles upward
out of the pile of flesh; brushes cloth,
hawk's wings, an angel with a horn;
or the others spread gaping mouths or legs, unborn
fish meat belly up, sucking their stumps,
eyes lit with speechless grief.

Or so it may be said at least.
Hieronymus, for your vision take
these shapings of the pregnant space.
But note you well, one of the fallen has hands like Michael's
one a fair face.

CERTAIN NOTES FROM BRUEGEL

CHILDREN'S GAMES

The houses float on their bright animal cries.
Children boil out of windows, round the doorways, down the streets
on stilts and each other's backs, in trains
riding the fences to Florence; the field
is full of children.

Where have they come from, pouring
without permission onto the canvas,
cheeky and wild?
And where did they get those coloured clothes, who said
they could take possession of the empty square?

Lumps of red and blue, rocking
on the grass, windmilling on the shore
hurl at heaven with their stubby hands.
Who said these children could be so unplanned?

CERTAIN NOTES FROM BRUEGEL

PEASANT DANCE

Maria is teaching Mayeken to dance
though Mayeken yet is not much more than a bundle of clothes
and even Maria at five
can dissolve at times into her grey dress.
The dancers gallop around them in earnest abandon
glad as the flags

beating the earth, swinging on coupled
arms and eyes.
The fat man pumps the bagpipes; Maria and Mayeken
hop in place, then twirl into the leg
of the table and smash a pot of beer
which pours over the earth and the black boots carry it
into the wheel and the spire.

Mayeken only
laughs and laughs.

CERTAIN NOTES FROM BRUEGEL

THE CRIPPLES

This for the ones misshapen
the legless, the one-eyed, the dumb
for the clump and the swing of the short sticks beating
the turf and the raucous faces
with their blobs of nose and tongue.
This for the one who rocks and the one who crawls
and the man in the tall red hat and colourful clothes who goes
no place at all.
A penny, a piece of bread, a picture on the wall.

O cripples, may your matters prosper.

CERTAIN NOTES FROM BRUEGEL

THE NUMBERING AT BETHLEHEM

As if it wasn't enough
hiking out here, dumb-footed in cracking boots,
losing the last of the firewood through the ice,
begging almost for cold pork, and then the wind,
now you tell me you're having dreams.

So something's going to happen. Well,
they're fighting over there, and I suppose that one
will go off with a bleeding nose —
is that the sort of thing you mean?
Then too, when we have stood in the snow for long enough,
we'll get a number so that we can go.
Rumour has it spring will someday come
and, if you don't watch where you're going, you'll collide
with the pregnant lady on the donkey.
Is that enough to keep your dreams content?

Look, your fingers are white.
Get by a fire, or wrap them in you cloak at least.
Maybe I'll find some hay where we can sleep tonight.

THE PINK BLOUSE

Always it seems quite random; a twist of light
or an unpredictable
flutter of atoms —
who knows
where absolute being will suddenly appear, or why
this one pink blouse should beat against my eyes
with all the griefs and joys of centuries?

Nor is there any possible response;
after all, I can hardly go
to a stranger and say, excuse me, your pink blouse
is tearing out my heart
is slicing through aorta, vena cava, pulmonary vein
with this incredible thrill
this incredible pain
of electricity and ice.
Or, I am flying on amazing wings
by reason of this piece of cloth (which is, as blouses go,
not even very nice)

This is not paradox, which makes
a sort of sense (I recognize
all figures of speech, the knowledge of the fool
the madman's awful rationality).
This is most clearly nonsense.

And sometimes
the purest gift must lie
in pure absurdity.

—————————— *PAT JASPER* ——————————

Pat Jasper was born in Teaneck, New Jersey, in 1943. She attended New Mexico State University where she was editor of "Puerto del Sol" literary magazine. She did graduate work at the University of Colorado. Pat moved to Canada in 1974. She is married, has three children, is currently conducting book discussion groups for the Council of Jewish Women, and hangs out in libraries a lot.

SUFFER YE THE CHILDREN

It was her last-ditch attempt
to appease the vestal virgins of her past,
enrolling me that first term at St. Francis of Assisi.
She must have known the jig was up,
that the secular step of her impious marriage
would trample any hope of keeping tradition alive.
She couldn't fight the world alone.

Still, she dressed me in tartan kilt and knee-socks,
placed a book-bag in one hand,
a lunch-box in the other,
and sent me off on her crusade.

Sister Augustine was the nun's name.
It was hard to pronounce
and meant nothing to me at the time.
Forgive me, Father, for I have sinned ...
Are confessions in order?

She seated us by test scores,
the bright ones on the front line,
the disgraced bringing up to the rear.
In later years, the impersonal ranks
of alphabetical order seemed a blessing.

She fired our surnames at us
and we fired back, disciplined as machine guns,
rattling off rote answers in our best catechismal chant.
Not "by heart." No, nothing to do with heart.

Deviation, not tolerated: retribution, swift.
The litany of a yard-stick cracked unyielding knuckles.

It was simply a question of time —

The day my turn came,
I left my lunch-box at school,
having only one usable hand,
and never went back for it.

Together we learned our lessons,
became one another's gods;
my mother's eyes resigned
as she bathed the welts on my small soul,
applied her soothing salve.

JUNE BUG

This morning as I was fixing lunch,
he tore through the screen door
looking for just-the-right-size box.
He had caught a frog in our window-well
and wanted to make a home for it.

I remembered June mornings
when I was eight in Oklahoma,
catching lizards, baby birds,
nesting them in just-the-right-size box,
adding rocks for boulders
       twigs for trees
          peanut-butter lids of water for ponds.
We tied strings around the legs of June bugs,
tethering them like buzzy green balloons.
In the evenings we would play
swinging statues until it got dark,
then catch fireflies,
shutting them up in mayonnaise jars
where they lit up pretend lanterns.

A peculiar penchant of eight-year-olds,
capturing creatures,
holding them close in sweaty palms,
stroking their bellies until they fall asleep.
To stop life long enough to touch it.
To keep it from escaping.

Does he clamp memories into boxes too?
Screw them inside jars,
sometimes forgetting to punch holes in the top
to let them breathe?

As I watch him through the curtains,
swatting flies to feed his frog,
I want to tie a string around his leg
and keep him eight forever.

IMPRINTS
(for my delinquent son)

When you were minutes old,
you blinked at your first mug-shot.
They inked the soles of your feet
and you made your first marks on the world.

A few years later
I loosened my grip
as you toddled off to another land
of fingerpaints and silhouettes,
a crew-cut innocence of up-turned noses
and slippery new feelings.

From the pages of your yearbook,
a sullen face I didn't recognize
clenched its square jaw,
the open stare closed
in misunderstanding
then disbelief
then anger.

Now the slap of a gavel
echoes that earlier slap
as you bury smudged hands
deep in your pockets.
I see only the back of your head.
Your footprints disappear down the hall.

INTIMATIONS

"Our noisy years seem moments in the being
Of the eternal Silence: truths that wake,
To perish never ..."
              Wordsworth

The subway surfaces
at the Davisville station
just long enough
for passengers to glimpse
        tombstones
hurrying by down Yonge Street.

In the blinking light,
a small boy stares
at his mother's lips.
His cocked head and puckered brow
disclose he has posed a question
and is absorbing her answer,
mouth slightly open,
a beige plug in his ear.

Deafened by the roll of the train,
we too watch her fish-lips and flexing fingers.
Their shapes confess she doesn't know
whether dead people like
being buried in cemeteries
or not.

Her implication
rises in his face
like a moon through fog,
unclear but ominous.

We stare at him staring
at her eyes this time.
She catches us —
We look away
too quickly to be casual.

Our eyes burrow back
into newspapers, paperbacks,
and the tunnels of ourselves.

UMBILICUS
(for my daughter)

In the predawn hours
before the birds begin to sing,
I can hear you
fluttering around your room,
sharpening pencils
setting up your easel
and I know the images
are flitting through your head too.
I wonder if my chirping words
scratched their way under your door
and woke you.
Or is there something in the air
drawing our thought formations
in the same southerly direction?
After breakfast I half expect
to open your door
and find my poem
nested in your canvas.

ELIZABETH JONES

Elizabeth Jones was born in South Africa, and has also lived in Scotland and France. She settled in Canada in 1966, and in Nova Scotia in 1970, where she lived for many years in the Annapolis Valley. She now lives in Halifax where she is doing graduate studies in French. She has published three volumes of poetry — "Castings", Fiddlehead, 1972; "Flux", Borealis, 1977; and "Nude on the Dartmouth Ferry", Black Moss, 1980. She is currently working on a book of popular history: "Gentlemen and Jesuits: First French Settlements in America, 1960-1613". Elizabeth has two daughters.

CHILD DRESSING

The landing stirs
with our morning movement.
As in a Dutch interior
a white doorway
frames the child dressing for school —
her long fair hair
brushes the stiff red and pink flowers
of the Oriental rug
as she bends to fasten her shoes.
Through the long window
a wild winter sun burns
catches her in its flow
through melting glass —
her profile a small centre
in its fierce rose.

LYING IN

Saturday
gusty March wind
early brightness
that stirs in the curtains. . . .

as I go past their door
my two daughters call to me sleepily —
we huddle into one bed
the window races with clouds
my eyes close on the sun
caught in the stark crotch of a tree. . . .

warm in the bed
they have cocooned with shawls
we drowse back into our different dreams. . . .

my arms around them
they are babies again
their lips nuzzle
they recede into me
in their arms
I am child
embryo —

secret as Stonehenge
in our circle of flesh
we are a timeless sleep of generations
in the sun. . . .

THANKSGIVING AT BLACK ROCK

The children are building pyramids
with smooth stones found on the beach.
We climb the new pine rungs
that strut raw up the rock.
Under the blue fall of sky
birch trees are light,
waving yellow skeleton leaves
ethereal in the sun.
Sheer down to the beach
cliff-face: its wicked facets
flash against the sea.

Waves pry restless
over the shore and the children
rebuild their pyramids
near old garbage pails
washed up with seaweed
by the last tide.

They break away, chasing each other
over the stones;
on one side
the sea sniffs blind and greedy
up the shore,
on the other
rocks sullenly conserve their tide-pools.

A sandpiper flits and runs
near a ridge of foam
belly quick white
in the sunlight.

The children's laughter reaches us
high as a shriek.

Our fingers tighten. . . .

TWO WOMEN

They have been absent
all winter from the screen
our window makes above the
kitchen sink — still for so long
with ice and thin trees
or scrambled with blizzards —
frame now for the ritual jerk
of the cock's quick head,
the determined amble of
the fifty-year old maiden daughter
her large pale arm
guiding the small crab shape
of her wandering mother
down the garden plot.

Spring   summer   fall
these two figures are solidly centre:
limbs wide or withered bent
over the clods of earth they
poke and prod and seed and weed
          and harvest.
Only the static of summer
thunderstorms can blur
them for us.

In the russet sunlight they
blink, triumphant with bushels of
tomatoes, beans and cucumbers — baskets high
               with the dead leaves they
                  burn in ditches
               cleansing the earth
                  for snow.

DAUGHTERS

Of course there are always
the photographs — their features
exactly and smilingly set
against vague branches and leaves
and they *jeunes filles en fleur*
caught between sunshine and rain —

yet somehow insubstantial
never as present
as these things they have left behind

straw hat
shadowing clear grey-green eyes
the small bump on a nose
that whitened bone-sharp
when she was tired

the shoes that contained
long ankles and feet and toes
the right foot flung out
at an angle
as she walked erect
down the drive

stronger than detergents or moth balls
the inalienable smells of their particular bodies
penetrate from dresses and tights and scarves
a sweater still holds
the wide curve of shoulders
above the piano

on old pencils and playing cards
in odd scraps of writing
I recognize the shape and pressure
of their hands

whether sitting or lying down
I don't have to close my eyes
to feel the distinct outline and weight
of two different heads
growing heavier
and lighter
on my arms.

———————— *DIANE KEATING* ————————

*Diane Keating was born in Winnipeg, graduated from the University of
Manitoba before moving to Rome, Italy, and Montreal. She now lives in
Toronto with her husband and children. Her first volume of poetry, ''In
Dark Places'', was published in 1978 by Black Moss Press. Her second
volume, ''No Birds or Flowers'', was published in 1982 by Exile Editions.*

MAD APPLES

Baba Yaga, Baba Yaga
by my belfry of ribs
my altar of hair
help me, My Lady of Lilies
lock me in stained glass
a chapel without doors.

> Daughters you must go to the suburbs
> wash on Mondays, arrange on Fridays.

Baba Yaga, Baba Yaga
by sweating shadow
bleeding cloud
help me, O Maid of Mad Apples
make the Prince blind
as the moon at midday.

> Daughter you must go to the malls
> consume the days . . .

Baba Yaga, Baba Yaga
by hood of hawks
skin of angels
help me, O Witch of the Wingless
to live behind glass
where gold light meets black air.

> My daughter you must go to the Prince.
> The tower is a bungalow on asphalt acres.
> The tower, your heart.

TWILIGHT TAPESTRY

4. Affirmation

Even then, waking
in the night
the simple song of poplars
broke my heart.
I'd peer through crib bars
to where mother sat
robed in ermine light.
In the hall
a perfect messenger,
the tall dark grandfather
clock ticking.
Even so, even then.

FECUNDITY

I'm a walled orchard.
Fruit swells
inflamed by the evening.

I ache for your bite,
to have water, fire,
sucked from me.
Outside the gates
I hear swans rutting.

I want to be pinned
to the hot earth,
my cry splitting
the moon, juice and seed.

God, how I long for stars
to mark where
I've taken you in.

BOTTOM OF THE GARDEN

God with his hump of pain
is ashamed in the sun.
I hear him
crouch in the shed,
his hand snailing
over the empty pots.

O Mother of Brown
make me scaly round,
blind as a bulb
in the winter ground.

The snake in his mouth
licks and flames.
The door clangs shut.
I am a clot of darkness:
shadows mimic questions.

O Mother of Stones
teach flowers to moan.
I learn to write
with chalk of bones.

——————————————— *JOY KOGAWA* ———————————————

Joy Kogawa, nee Nohayania, was born in Vancouver B.C., in 1935. Her published works include "The Splintered Moon", 1967; "A Choice of Dreams", Fiddlehead, 1974; "Jericho Road", McClelland & Stewart, 1977; and "Obasan", Penguin, 1981 (David Godini in U.S. and Futami Shobo in Japan). "Obasan" won Books in Canada First Novel Award, Canadian Authors' Prose Fiction Award, and Before Columbus Foundation's American Book Award.

JULY IN COALDALE

July in Coaldale and
so hot the scalp steams
and I am curling my mother's
fine white hair with her
new mist curler iron
I bought for her
81st birthday and
she is telling me
of her early morning dream
that it was Christmas and
there was music, I can't
remember the song, she says
but after a few more curls
she is singing in Japanese
"Joy to the world"
somewhat out of tune
because she is deaf now
and her throat is dry but
she was famous for her
singing once and
she says in her dream
there was an old dry plant
that started to bloom

BIRD POEM

when deidre was so angry she
could only droop with it after
hitting the wall so hard she said
her hand was broken and i
could hardly remember that much
helplessness and rage

i am prepared for many forms
of farewell, but this? a
bandaged wing, a wild bird,
my fifteen year old high school girl

i wait without push or pull
through rage and flight and
unexpected landings as wearily
as did my parents with their
long distance night praying
their interlocking cage of arms
an invisible flexible net and nest

SAITH NUAH

saith nuah
holding her symbols
the dove
the olive branch
saith nuah
ancient babylonian
goddess of floods

build friendships
well oiled ships
take feathers
from my dove
make vessels for flood times
sail the higher ways
of love

─────────── *ROSALIND MacPHEE* ───────────

Rosalind MacPhee was born in Summerland, B.C., in 1946. She was educated at U.B.C.. Her published works include "Scarecrow", Fiddlehead, 1979; "Magpie", Coach House Press, 1980; and "What Place is This?" Coach House Press, 1983. Rosalind has just returned from Europe where she completed research for a new work in progress. She has two daughters.

NARES LAKE

Rivers stitch one lake to another.
Jessie measures
the expertise of a woman's fingertips
at petit point. Time
at its frame.
Unused thread on her lap.
Watches her flashing needle
pick up intricate whorls of pattern
as she threads her way in
and out. Her thoughts
inward. Enmeshed in a reverie
too fine to thread.
She pulls her needle up
out of the fabric. Carrying colours of sky
and mountains. Catches a stitch here,
there. *I was.*
I am, Who knows. Which
is which.
Everything stitched
in the hell that is real, silent,
no one is prepared
to fix eyes upon . . . that . . .
a map of a distant land
where Jessie's son sleeps on secrets.
The horizon runs through her eyes.
Thread through a needle.

DECOY

It is at times
as if my homecoming were really
unexpected, it is
my children and a huge emptiness,
it is the voice
of my mother
calling me back,
calling me to be still
like winterseed
or despair:
it is her last hours
where she slept white-faced to the wall
a superstition
or a threat: the dawn hovering
her enormous shadow
above my bed
growing larger, closing
around my memory of her
alone, reaching to me
saying to me, *goodbye*
be still
you'll soon know your children's absence
you'll soon
be coming towards me
you are already in sight.

MORNING

It's that feeling
of not knowing when things
will begin, of your nerves having
split ends
          of sorting through experiences
collected
and stacked
like forgotten firewood
                    regurgitating
on how your son
              finding woman
has stopped writing letters home
    your daughter
                  finding man
has started.

─────── *SUSAN McMASTER* ───────

*Susan McMaster's poetry has appeared in, among others, "Event",
"Grain", "Quarry", "Arc", "Rideau River Anthology", and "Los".
"Pass this way again", a collection of performance poetry and poetry with
composer A. McClure, has recently been published by Underwhich Editions
(1983); as has a pamphlet, "Seven poems", by Ouroboros (1983).
"Haiku" with composer D. Parsons, is forthcoming from Ouroboros
(1983). Susan McMaster was the founding editor of "Branching Out"
magazine. She has hosted "Sparks 2", and Ottawa Poetry Show; and is the
Ottawa representative of "Quarry. As well, she performs and creates with
FIRST DRAFT, an Ottawa intermedia group. Recent shows include
several appearances on television and radio, and productions at Theatre
2000, the A.K.A. Gallery (Saskatoon), the Axle Tree Coffee House
(Toronto), and SAW Gallery (Ottawa, forthcoming).*

THE READING ENDS AT NINE

You leave the house
on a legitimate excuse —
a reading at the library

You take the car
and as you drive, consider
    a warm-windowed restaurant
    full of plush corners,
    the dusky park
    with its promenade,
    your old lover's house
    with its wine and blue door

But you don't touch the brake
and arrive at the reading
on time, and as surely
as if your toddler were strapped
in the harness behind
and your baby sleeping
in the GM Lov-seat

You enjoy the reading
moderately — the mustachioed poet
praises Tinkerbell's thighs,
then pauses to remark
on the 'really good poets'
who are 'mothers and wives'

Then you leave the library
promptly at nine,
drive, without pausing
back past the restaurant,
back past the park,
back past the blue door,

and arrive duly home
at nine-seventeen.

You hang your coat
over your daughter's parka,
put down your program
and pick up the teapot
to empty dregs
of afternoon gossip
into the sink

when your husband looks up
from the Expos and says
"You're back awfully early.
Was the reading that dull?"

        Tell me,
        did you really throw
        the teapot at the wall?

and when the crash wakes the baby
and your husband backs

from you   to her

        Tell me,
        do you bend
        and start to
        pick up pieces?

THREE WOMEN CAMPING

In the night
men's voices
veer toward the tent
lantern light careers
across canvas

Grandmother
thirty years of
bulwark against
poison/traffic/rape
scrabbles for glasses

Mother
twenty-seven years of
thoughtless sleep
and three of fear
jerks up
pulls on jeans
her bushman's shirt
reaches for the tent flap

Inside, daughter
three years of
dreams
brushes a spider
off her face
rolls onto her back

    arms and legs
    open
    to the voices
    the lantern
    and the
    easeful night

SPRING OVER GROWN

On a sudden thirty spring
the trees are intricate
rough combs
their budding mesh
demanding attention
exclamation

This year I turn irritably from
the bare tangled fuss
of seasonal expectation

      from
      also
      your intricate
      forehead

ANNIVERSARY

Fucking in the afternoon
tempts the gods —

The baby's asleep,
the child at school,
the plumber come and gone
(reminding us to clean our pumps)

We draw the curtains,
lock the doors,
pull off jeans and shirts,
release
a whole day's
muskiness
        but
as scent
welcomes warmth

the telephone rings.

He answers,
I lie back, hopeful
on the couch
but

        the doorbell peals
        waking the baby
        who starts to cry, as
        down the street
        the schoolbell rings,
        and Mother's on the phone
        (if I have a minute)

So I pick up the phone,
he unlocks the door,
pays the paperboy,
brings down the baby,
opens the curtains
and

the last chance
of afternoon love
gone

    we share instead
    a cup of tea.

———————— *SHARON H. NELSON* ————————

Sharon H. Nelson was born in Montreal and has lived there most of her life. She has worked as a journalist, editor, and has taught creative writing at Concordia University and at the University of British Columbia. Her publications include "Mad Women & Crazy Ladies" (Sunken Forum Press, 1983), and "Blood Poems" (Fiddlehead Poetry Books, 1978). She is the author if numerous reports and articles, including "Bemused, Branded, and Belittled: Women and Writing in Canada," which was published in "Fireweed" 15 (December 1982). Sharon H. Nelson is currently Managing Editor of Metonym Productions, a company that specializes in technical literature. She is also a partner in the Feminist Research and Editorial Group.

A FOOTSTOOL IN HEAVEN

> According to the Talmud, the reward of a good
> Jewish wife is that she will be her husband's
> footstool in heaven.

Today is moving day.
Today
all the parcels and possessions of my life
are loaded into a van and I
will sleep in an airport motel,
await the early call to rise
and travel two thousand miles to be
a Jewish wife.

Today the children are not happy.
They are strained, tired, bored, unsettled.
I have no strength left after packing boxes
to console anyone for losses,
to comfort or to reassure.

And I'm telling you
if those kids run through the new house
the way they've run through this one
I will tie a rope up every six feet in every room in that house.
I will make holes in the walls; I will hammer nails in;
I will put ropes between the nails;
every six feet, every six feet,
ropes in every room of that house.

Today, like yesterday or Monday or
all the days of my life
my husband sits in his big chair
and watches the hired men, the children,
the whole performance. I am counting.

I am counting the money we will pay the hired men
because my husband sits in his big chair.
I am counting the money I might have
if someone had helped with the packing.
I am counting the number of boxes I have packed,
the number the hired men have packed.
I am counting.

I am counting the hours I will work
to make the money to buy the things the children will need
that we can't afford because we gave the money to the hired
men for packing boxes
because my husband sits in his big chair.

I am counting. I do not lose track.
I am counting. I did mathematics at university and
I am counting. I can still count.

I count everything: hairpins, toothbrushes, boxes, grapes,
apples, insults. I do not lose track of anything and
I do not stop counting.

HORTICULTURE

Unkempt as tulips after a spring storm,
we huddle, housebound, shamed by our shapes;
bulges, contours, crevices, our shame,
each inch examined and appraised, stung
by the slick tip of fashion's whip
that tames the body as it tunes the mind.

We are
grown
for this:
to learn
our
ugliness.

Decorative, straight-backed things,
we learn the art of forcing:
paperwhites at Christmas, long-stemmed, tall,
the Easter lily on her stalk,
all virginal.

Displayed like hothouse plants,
we turn and bend,
slender as an iris stem.

Underfed,
we glow
bright with fever,
discipline,
take
less and less,
each meal a self-inflicted wound.

Hungry,
we do not
bleed.

Sterile,
we bloom.

FARM REPORT

1

imagine if i'd stayed
milking jenny, boiling mash for the sow,
one ear cocked always to the sound of the weather;

imagine if i'd stayed
in overalls, my rings boxed neatly
in the right-hand dresser drawer, my wedding dress
hung neatly in the plastic garment bag
in the spare room cupboard,
imagine if i'd stayed;

the cuts the hay makes on your fingers,
the marks the man lays on your arm when he
pulls you to him,
the marks that fade, that you forget
year in and year out when the other side of the bed's
as close as you get
and you begin to wonder if maybe the sun's
bleached your hair and roughed your skin so much that no one
not even the passing through hired man would want. . .

imagine if i'd stayed

FARM REPORT

2

the house was big, 12 rooms i
kept and swept, always had oatmeal
cookies for the kids; the neighbour's kids all
ran away from home to sit
at the big oval table in the kitchen

i had a stool there for my feet, built low,
just under the table so i could sit and sew
or shell beans and peas; it's
hard on the back hour after hour, day in, day out;
and the peace
of seeing the sun set out the big window

it was
hard
to leave

FARM REPORT

3

i don't know quite when it was
john turned against me;
it wasn't so much against at first as
from; after the children. . .
after the children john complained
about everything; i think now maybe he was
jealous of the time i had to spend;
and being so tired all the time,
what with the pigs and the milking and driving machines
and we had chickens then, i guess maybe
i was too tired to notice much

year in and year out his back turned; it wasn't
normal; i know i
ought to have suspected something;
maybe i did, deep down, too tired to care,
tired all the time, but then i thought
it must be another woman, another woman someplace,
maybe one of the towns, but
i was wrong

FARM REPORT

4

i think sometimes i should have stayed;
sometimes i think of that big kitchen,
the bigness of the table in the bigness of the kitchen;
sometimes i think my grandmother was right,
that's woman's lot, to stay and stay and stay it out

sometimes i just wonder, wonder what got into me,
what pulled me out; no pushing would have done,
but when i realized what it was with john. . .
and worrying about the children, i
just moved

FARM REPORT

5

i used to wonder, when i was back there,
when the house was filled with light,
wonder how people could abide those small city apartments;
i used to wonder, who lives in just one room?

you get used to it, get used to almost anything,
used, almost, to the idea of
anything;
it's the idea that hurts

FARM REPORT

6

sometimes john turns up across the street;
he'll stand hour after hour, watching this place;
or sometimes i'll get a tape in the mail,
my own voice on the phone; i don't know how he
does it; the man owns fifteen guns; i
know i ought to do something about it. . .but
i can't think what

FARM REPORT

7

at night, sleeping isn't easy;
the noises are wrong; it takes so long
to adjust that small internal clock
that tells the hours by the sun
the weather by the wind and just
gets confused by traffic

nobody comes here; the place is small and
really john might turn up anytime;
and it isn't safe to stand against the light,
not even with the curtains drawn

i think, sometimes, at night, of the big house,
the sounds there, and the thickness of the dark;
i sit here in this narrow room and grieve;
the loneliness is a sharp-toothed thing

the loneliness is
a mouse eating a shoe;
you always think
it couldn't happen to you

—JANIS RAPOPORT—

Janis Rapoport was born in Toronto in 1946. Educated in Canada and Switzerland, she is a graduate in philosophy from New College, University of Toronto. She lived and worked in London, England from 1967-70. She now lives with her husband and four children in Toronto. Janis has published 3 volumes of poetry, one play, and was co-editor of "Landscape" (poetry) and co-author of "Imaginings". In addition, her poetry, plays and critical writings have appeared in magazines, anthologies and newspapers and have been broadcast on C.B.C. Radio.

CHILD'S DRAWING WITH CRAYON
for Sara Seager (my daughter)

Today, for the first time,
you drew me:
purple, curly hair,
straight red limbs,
legs that grow out of chins,
arms, elongated ears.

Looking out of a window square
within the shingles clipped
by yellow locks:
eyes without irises,
pupilled by red veins swirling
against the white;
hollow and proud, the
hair hat busy on my head;
the matchsticked legs and arms
leave a torso quite invisible:
you have seen me as
I really am.

THE GREEN TENT
  for Renata Donegani

Under the green tent
no shadows ring the sterile light.
The air is numb. A Chopin *Nocturne* pulses through,
pre-wound in acrylic-spool beats. The red secondhand
accelerates around the clock without numbers
and I cannot walk: my wrists and ankles are bound,
gold ropes. People gather. Instruments trace
delicate shapes then plunge, mixing my blood with the light.
The crowd walks across my skin, heavily footprinting
bone after bone.

In the green tent
death pokes a finger through the bandaged air
anxious to pluck a New Year's fruit.
They forgot to clean the canvas and my mouth
is too parched to speak. I know we are
in the desert where the sun has bleached
the rainbow white. I can see the cactus prickles
glitter although I cannot open my eyes.

In the green tent of death
I cannot scream, cannot weep
not yet, not yet. The juggle of halos,
the clock with no face, the masked crowd,
the dazzle of needles and the floating light.

Her first cry
ripples the music into her own melody:
her newborn voice dancing down the light.

Death surrenders the crown to birth.
Death retreats carefully into the canvas folds as they fall.
Death stitches a tent green shadow onto the hospital wall.

THE STRAWBERRY NIGHT
for Helen Weinzweig

Through the strawberry night your mother comes.
Crystal pendants hang in her eyes, reflecting the oval rain.
Chalk purls her hair with each electric pattern in the sky.
Under an umbrella she carries a white bundle in one arm.

We sit among the wild strawberry plants of our neighbour
enjoying the protection of the moon for our feast.
Her long narrow garden is strewn with manure and hay,
like a field. Some of the plants she has bagged in plastic
in order, she says, to create a greenhouse effect.
Others ride the wind and the rain,
tossing their ripening bells.
At our backs, the peaceful red and yellow back of the brick house,
the stained glass window and white gingerbread trim on the roof.
It is from this direction your mother approaches.
The lightning rod captures a flash, directing its energy
into the ground along a path beneath our feet.

Your mother arives.
She places the bundle, a sleeping infant, among the strawberries
and begins to speak.

We look at each other, you and I,
hoping at least one of us has understood. I get up,
pushing my chair aside through the mud, gesturing
for her to rest while I go look for my father
whom I hope will be able to translate.

But my father is on a city street, in sunlight,
awarding medals to small boys who resemble his son and
grandson but are not. He says he cannot leave the city.

I am tired when I return.
The spectre I thought was your mother sits alone.
As I approach, she turns and bends to gather
the fallen strawberries. She hurls them into the sunrise.

A shower of red bursts across my chest.

IMPRESSIONS OF LOVE ON EASTER SUNDAY MORNING
for Renata Donegani (my daughter)

As we fall asleep, the sun rays through our window, striping
the walls with its rainbows, and after, castles form in the shadows.
The baby welcomes the rainbows and castles with a concert
of chatter. Six cats arrive at the bedroom door. Marmalade presents
his whiskers. His orange pin striped business suit has been sent
to the cleaners. He pushes his naked paws between the jamb and the floor.
Brahms fails to lullabye the baby who is waltzing in her crib and
shaping the air into wands and swords for the castles. A black heart
startles me. Engraved at last night's community dance, it now begins
to beat on my hand. The baby breakfasts on peaches and pablum;
sunspots freckle her pewter spoon. Our self-portraits glare back at us
from a ceiling of mirrors and the gray eyes of the baby
refuse to consider sleep. The cats paw the stairs into up-escalators
and we cannot get down to the kitchen where hydrangeas and lillies
bloom on the table. The charosets and matzo lie there uneaten.
The toy koala bear begins to somersault along the bars of the crib,
from frustration or perhaps to prevent hysterical laughter. An octopus
with polkadot tentacles attempts to wrap sleep around the baby
who is playing Brahms again, this time mixing the metal notes
of the mobile with bird prayer and flower song and the church bells
of Easter. You balance the baby on your sunwarm shoulders, peaches
and pablum lace your beard and your back. The baby confers with
the marmalade cat as he shifts gear from purr to meow and sharpens
his claws on the door. The knitted clown rubs his eyes,
removes his purled hat, sends a shell boat drifting into the morning.
The sunrise spins the room into colours. The tinned lullabies break
with our laughter. (Whoever invented sleep has forgotten.)
Love escapes through a crack in the door, balancing down the stairs
on its back, between the hopes of the gray-eyed baby and
the purrs of the marmalade cat.

———— *ROBYN SARAH* ————

Robyn Sarah was born in New York in 1949. She grew up in Montreal and studied at McGill University and at the Quebec Conservatoire of Music. In 1976 she co-founded (with her husband Fred Louder) Villeneuve, a Montreal small press operating out of their home. Robyn teaches at Champlain Regional College. She has two children. Her two books of poetry are "The Space Between Sleep and Waking", Villeneuve, 1981, and "Shadowplay", Fiddlehead Poetry Books, 1978.

TIDES

After nine months
of strangely equal days, then ten
clocked by the press and flood
of milk, her child
eats fruit with his fingers
and scrambles after her, hands pulling her skirt.
Seasons have changed
and she hasn't noticed. One day
she woke up, and it was fall —
another, the snow was melting;
always she fell back
into the close dream where his little face
was sun and moon.
Now, like a young girl, wide-eyed
in the sudden light of outside
she feels it begin
again — like the end
of a sleep she never would have thought
possible, like the waking
of a stopped pulse ticking the world
back into being. Familiar
as an old tune, but this time felt
with a new vibration, the echo
of that huge splash upon whose ripples
she has been riding — it comes again:
the downward tug of the blood
at full moon,
amazing as the sound
of the first rain.

CAT'S CRADLE

When women together sit sipping
cold tea and tugging at the
threads of memory, thoughtfully
pulling at this
or that bit or loop, or slipping
this loop over that finger till
warp and weft of past lives begin
crazily to unwind, when women sit
smoking and talking, the talk
making smoke in the air, when they shake
shreds of tobacco out of a crumpled pack
and keep drinking the same weak tea
from the same broken pot, something clicks
in the springs of the clock
and it's yesterday again,
and the sprung yarn rolls down loose
from the spool of the moon.

When women together sit talking
an afternoon, when they talk
the sun down, talk stars, talk
dawn — they talk up a dust
of sleeping dogs and bones
and they talk a drum for the dust
to dance to, till the dance
drums up a storm; when women
sit drumming fingers on tops
of tables, when the tables turn
into tops that spin and hum
and the bobbin of the moon
keeps spinning its fine yarn down

to catch fingers, when fingers catch
talk in a cat's cradle, and turn
talk into a net to catch the curve
of the storm — then it's talk
against talk, till the tail
of the storm trails into dust
and they talk the dust back down.

Things that matter and don't matter
are caught together, things done and undone,
and the kettle boils dry and over
while they lean closer to peer down
into the murky water where last night's dream
flicks its tail and is gone
(and the reel of the moon keeps cranking
its long line down), when women together
sit sipping cold tea and sawing on the strings
of memory, it is an old tune.
The rice sticks to the bottom of the pan
and things get left out in the rain.

MAINTENANCE

Sometimes the best I can do
is homemade soup, or a patch on the knee
of the baby's overalls.
Things you couldn't call poems.
Things that spread in the head,
that swallow
whole afternoons, weigh down the week
till the elastic's gone right out of it —
so gone
it doesn't even snap when it breaks.
And one spent week's
just like the shapeless bag
of another. Monthsful of them,
with new ones rolling in and
filling up with the same junk: toys
under the bed, eggplant slices sweating
on the breadboard, the washing machine
spewing suds into the toilet, socks
drying on the radiator and falling down
behind it where the dust lies furry and
full of itself . . . The dust!
what I could tell you about
the dust. How it eats things —
pencils, caps from ballpoint pens,
plastic sheep, alphabet blocks.
How it spins cocoons
around them, clumps up and
smothers whatever strays into
its reaches — buttons,
pennies, marbles — and then
how it lifts, all of a piece,
dust-pelts
thick as the best velvet
on the bottom of the mop.
                              Sometimes
the best that I can do
is maintenance: the eaten
replaced by the soon-to-be-eaten, the raw

by the cooked, the spilled-on
by the washed and dried, the ripped
by the mended; empty cartons
heaved down the cellar stairs, the
cans stacked on the ledge, debris
sealed up in monstrous snot-green bags
for the garbage man.

And I'll tell you what
they don't usually tell you: there's no
poetry in it. There's no poetry
in scraping concrete off the high chair tray
with a bent kitchen knife, or fishing
with broomhandle behind the fridge
for a lodged ball. None in the sink
that's always full, concealing its cargo
of crockery under a head
of greasy suds. Maybe you've heard
that there are compensations? That, too's
a myth. It doesn't work that way.
The planes are separate. Even if there are
moments each day that take you by the heart
and shake the dance back into it, that you lost
the beat of, somewhere years behind — even if
in the clear eye of such a moment you catch
a glimpse of the only thing worth looking for —
to call this compensation, is to demean.

The planes are separate. And it's the
other one, the one called maintenance,
I mostly am shouting about.
I mean the day-to-day,
that bogs the mind, voice, hands
with things you couldn't call poems.
I mean the thread that breaks.
The dust between
typewriter keys.

CHARLENE SHEARD

Charlene Sheard was born in Toronto, and is a graduate of York University in Women's Studies. She is actively involved in women's writing in Toronto and has been published in several periodicals. She is currently studying part-time and works as program co-ordinator in a small community centre in Toronto. She makes an annual trek to the east coast where she does most of her writing.

my mother takes tea

i rise early
to have tea alone
look out at the sun
and find
sitting below the window
my mother
there in the garden
sipping tea
alone

she is motionless
except for the act of
bringing the cup to her lips
she is staring out
at the river/the fields
pensive and quiet
i do not recall this
part of her before now
excited to share
our mutual habit
i open my mouth
to call her
she begins to hum.......

my mother takes tea
in the garden

alone.......

my father

for the first time
you refer to me as
a woman
not a young lady
a girl
your child/but
a woman
i waited 30 years
to grow up for you
to be accepted as
a member of your world
finally equal

you tell your friends
that i am my own person
you respect me
for my decisions
love me/but
i am no longer
your 'child'

i have grown up.

i waited 30 years
to hear this
and now,
i want to climb up
on your lap
cry my sadness
into your chest
have you tell me
it will be different
when i grow up.

i watch your knarled fingers
separate the earth and
gently lay each bulb in its bed
like newborn babies.
you know they'll grow with care
bright and beautiful.

you rise
take my face in your knotted hands
and kiss me
then,
with satisfaction on your face,
you lead me by the hand into lunch.

i don't think i ever really minded
your aging
in fact
that was quite wonderful
yet i   grew to hate
the passing of years
as they robbed you of
your magnificent hands.

it doesn't disturb you though
or prevent you
from doing anything
i have learned
to accept so much through you
for that
i love you

to you
those misplaced joints
each have a sory
each story
you animate to my wonderment

   i will always be a child
   to their tales.

——————————CAROLYN SMART——————————

Carolyn Smart was born in England in 1952. Her publications include
"Swimmers in Oblivion" (York Publishing, 1981) and "Power Sources"
(Fiddlehead Poetry Books, 1982). She lives in Elginberg, Ontario, where
she is currently at work on a new manuscript entitled "Stoning the Moon",
acting as regional representative for "Fireweed: A Feminist Quarterly", and
writing a regular column on craft for "Poetry Canada Review".

FLYING
(for Mary di Michele)

All our lives they've said we expect too much
from what bone and the spark of cells
will make of a simple life
Two of us so eager for the future we imagine
we smoke the air for speed
anything to get what we want   perfection
Believe we can change the world
with language   a tool to call down the stars
watch them come   eager puppies   to the page
You are I are reckless
wanting to believe in everything
a planet of kindness

Your hand on my arm at a party
touches beyond our public selves
past false conversation   clink of glass on wood
stories people tell of their lives
later thinking *why did I say so much*
who will hurt me
but your hand is saying to me
Care   Imagine   Believe
touching the way women touch each other
for comfort   for rest
This from your small hand   trust
the world we desire

For your birthday I give you a gathering of friends
never expecting the gift you will give
Not knowing you change me forever you say
once   everybody could fly
bright eyes   arms in the air as you talk
saying this perhaps for the first time
with such ease my eyes fill up
relief of shared vision
You a small child clinging to steep rock
head already part of the sky
holding on so tight because you know
with only one brief gesture you could fly
without even trying   floating
only a step away   not surprised by this
not afraid   your concern only for your mother nearby
who has forgotten all she knew about flight
knows terror   you hold onto the earth
choose this   still believe
Once you say to us *everybody could fly*

Then you sit back   hands still   face glowing
Four other voices remember dreams and Peter Pan
I could have said
waiting for the light to change
the steering wheel solid in my hands
I saw trees about to burst open
clouds moving too fast above the city
and then I knew what I'd always known
if I just let go the air would take me
I thought I was at the edge of madness
felt the sky pulling and thought it wanted my soul
knew it would be so easy   *but I held on*

I could have said
again and again it happens
I feel the speed of the planet
as it rolls through space   *such silence*
the ground under my feet gives up gravity
clouds begin their whirl
I know this all so well   *one more step*
and I would be   *flying*

My deepest secret
fear always in the telling
what if they banished me   put me away
like children with golden eyes who practice levitation
some kind of science fiction or madness
the terror of misunderstanding
You have taken the loneliness of silence from me
with your need to believe
in what this world could be

Bone and the spark of cells
is all we have ever had
We see so clearly what we want
from a simple life
Language and touch bring us closer
to what we once knew before fear
The belief in tenderness   innocence
Remember   one more step and then
the air

OUTSIDE GRAND FORKS, NORTH DAKOTA

We smoke cigarettes and the time passes slowly.
As I am driving, you are doing the talking
and in between, we listen to the radio.
Franco is dead the radio says
and outside, it is thirty below zero,
and the beaten wheat is lying in the fields.
There are no trees here.
The road is long and straight
and the cigarettes seem to last forever.

We are lonely for each other
as we drive along, we are lonely
for even ourselves.
We reach the building we are aiming for,
a low white building lying in the shade
of the cold afternoon.
We sit in the crowded waiting room,
the smell of dust on the magazines, the plastic plants.
From time to time the nurse passes by,
an opaque jar in her hands.
Somewhere a girl is screaming,
but no one in the room is listening,
and I cannot talk to you
because it is you who will be screaming
and I'm just here to listen.

You've gone in — I cannot bear to remember
the look we give each other
before you turn the short corner and are gone.
It doesn't take long,
and suddenly I see what it is
that the nurse is carrying,
and she passes me by with this thing in her hands
and she flushes it down the toilet.

I can hear them saying *bring me a bowl,*
she's going to be sick
but you weren't — you were always too proud.
There's your pale face coming towards me,
my arms around your fine body.

Oh my sweet friend
we are lonely for even our childhoods
as we drive towards Canada,
the wind chilling right to our bones.

MIRIAM WADDINGTON

Miriam Waddington was born in Winnipeg, and educated in that city, Ottawa, Toronto and Philadelphia. She has a professional degree in Social Work (MSW), an academic one in English (M.A.), and an honorary doctorate (D.Litt.). After working as a case worker in child guidance clinics, hospitals, prisons, family and children's agencies in Toronto and Montreal, and as a teacher of Social Wrok during the forties and fifties, she changed professions and now teaches English and Canadian Literature at York University in Toronto where she holds the rank of Professor. Miriam Waddinton has published eleven books of poetry, is the author of a critical study of A.M. Klein, and has edited the critical work of John Sutherland and ''The Collected Poems of A.M. Klein.'' In addition she has published dozens of critical articles and reviews, short stories and translations of both prose and poetry from Yiddish and German. Some of her own work has been translated and published in the Soviet Union, Hungary, Japan, Romania, and South America.

NIGHT IN OCTOBER

(THE dream, the dream, where did it begin?
In the downpour of light that flooded through the sky?
Where was the key that opened up the door
To a white room with candles burning?)

At midnight the wind
Stretched long leathery fingers
Against the warm night,
Lifted the roof of torment and sang
Lullabies from an old book
Of apples and nutmegs and peacocks that flew
Ceaselessly circling a golden sea.
(It was dream, it was dream,
Light echoed and keys were lost in the sea.)

The pain came with its symphony
With its many players
Who tuned forceps and scissors
And the sharp cruel dancers
Who whirled and galloped
All over my girlhood, shipwrecked and bitter.
(There was an answer, I heard it through water
Through the coils and columns,
But it was lost in the weather
The genesis of snow.)

The dream the dream
That nested like a dove
In evergreens and eaves
That fed on angel honey
And loaves of silky bread,
The dream still nameless,
Wandering and restless,
Searching for me.

I in my torment was chained to the moment,
Heard the harsh rasp of wire
And the ring of steel
On vast white porcelain —
All over the prairie my prayers were empty,
All over the ocean my hands had spread
And the doctors were dancing

Fandangoes, boleros,
They sang commands in a chorus
Of feverish laughter, "Once more and again,"
"And now die again, yes die, yes die,"
So I died just to please them.

(But the dream, the dream, where did it begin?
In jewels, in stars, in powdery snow
Or sin? Oh lullabies be quiet and still,
The dandelions do die and on my graveyard green
Their white petticoats of lace upon the hilltop blow,
And pebbles bleached and dry
Neatly line the path.)

From far away a voice
Calls me from the dead,
"Are you there, are you there,
Are you there?" Urgently jolted
Out of death without warning
I wake to the new child's crying.
It is morning, morning —
Full of problems and sorrow.

(Light fades from the window,
And the dream, nameless and wandering
Goes to sleep in its echoes
Unsolved and insoluble.)

LOSING MERRYGOROUNDS

My longago childpark
my everwas merrygoround
twicelost are you
in circuses and suburbs
lost now my teetertotters,
thin tensioners
over the crushed grasses
my broken mintstems lost
and silkgreen ferns lost

where my hands first
foraged in   where my
footsteps stirred   light-
dappled under trees that
sheltered me like fathers
where my eyelids were
touched   kissed longago
by sun's parentfingers
now dry now hermited
parchmented bookstacked
and exiled now from
my longago merrygoround
my talltreed childpark
twice have I lost them
once
left behind in the
shadowcity of my child
years and after wandering
lost lost again in my own
outpacing children

outpaced by them
the spring has blinked
me open first watercarried
then almost flowered me
but a dry bud am I un-
dappled now and pitiless,
neverblooming but schooled
I suppose in the how
of losing merrygorounds
and the careful prose
of growing up.

THE TERRARIUM

In the terrarium
with the snakes and worms
the small mona lisa goes
her path is involute
a melancholy track where
mosses part and close
their secret forests
to let her through.

Here seashells loom
like humpy mountains
and in her path the
small mint quivers
an aromatic wind;
the steep air stirs
a fern uncoils a yawn
and fiercely shakes its stem
so a torrential rain of spores
breaks on her head.

And still she smiles
no weather is dangerous
in her glass garden,
lost in the jungle steam
she treads moist mushroom paths
and trails the sound
of crumbling leaf mould,
she's silent as the dust.

At night the child dreams
of the small mother
he has captured there,
of world's darkness tamed
and reduced to garden size
where a smiling mona lisa
as small as snakes or worms
is circling all the paths.

The child sleeps on; his
light wand touches glass
and wakes the magic stones;
then with a waxen touch he
commands the mountains kneel
and tells the worms to speak.

THE TRANSPLATED:
SECOND GENERATION

Some day my son
you'll go to Leningrad,
you'll see grey canals
under arches and bridges,
you'll see green and white
walls of winter palaces,
you'll visit the towered
prison across the river
and smell the breath
of dead revolutions;
perhaps you'll even hear
the ghostly marching of
sailors in empty avenues
and catch the ebbing sound
of their wintry slogans.

You'll remember
that Jews could spend no
nights in Leningrad when
it was called St. Petersburg;
Jews moved with documents
shuffled and crushed like
paper; the Yiddish writer
Peretz was met by his friend
Anski at Leningrad station;
he delivered his lecture
to a crowded hall then spent
the night in a suburb
twenty miles away.

Some day my son
when you are in Leningrad
you'll see those palaces
and turning fountains,
you'll stare at pendulums
of gilded saintliness,
count kingly treasure-hoards

in glass museum-cases;
then you'll remember
Nova Scotia's pasture lands
its clumps of blueberries
and our August mornings
on hidden lakes at the end
of logging roads.

And some day my son
just there in Leningrad
across those distances
You will feel my Winnipeg:
its lakes of fish its skies
of snow and its winds of
homelessness will stir
something in your blood;
then will you hear forgotten
languages and you will read
the troubled map of our
long ancestral geography
in your own son's eyes.

THE WHEEL

How does the seed grow
in what city is the wheel
that turns the world,
Montreal or Winnipeg?
We do not know.

The best we know
is like the child asleep,
helpless, a face
with sorrows deep, the best
we have is that we're partly
old and partly young but

Best there is,
and this best we give:
to nature's question
our answer is:
turn the world and
shelter us, the wheel
is in the seed.

—————————— *BRONWEN WALLACE* ——————————

Bronwen Wallace lives in Kingston, Ontario. Her most recent book, "Signs of The Former Tenant", appeared from Oberon in 1983. She was the winner of the National Magazine Award for Poetry in 1980 and is also a sometime film maker. Her documentary "All You Have To Do (co-directed with Chris Whynot) won a Red Ribbon at the American Film Festival in 1982.

DREAMS OF RESCUE

In the dream
the car is a sound,
a screech of brakes that tears a hole
in the sunlight, big enough
for the dog to flop through, fish-like
guts spilling on the side of the road.

In the dream
the children's voices
crying *do something   do something*
are a mist I grope through, fingers thick
as my tongue with the smell of dust and blood.

A telephone grows from my hand
and my cry for help recedes into the churn
and whining of machinery
that rings
and rings
and rings
me into 3 a.m. darkness, cold
floor under my feet
and your voice
coming at me from the coast.

"Pour yourself a drink," you say
"I'm paying."

It's only midnight where you are
two hours into a bottle and your second
pack of cigarettes, but there's no use arguing
and somehow the scotch I pour
cuts through time zones and prairie winters
until night and distance
are another room in this house
we are learning to build: two women
sitting up late, sharing out our days
with the whiskey and the cigarettes.

*

Something has happened to you.
In your voice it's a kind of tenderness
that hovers over your words — like a mother
watching her kid learn to walk —
as if you could protect them
from what they must say.

You're telling me what you're reading
these days, titles I recognize, names.
Each one flares for a moment, struck match
that pulls some reassuring object
— watch face, ashtray, scotch bottle —
out of the darkness
where your face bobs, white and scared.

Little sister.
When you were three
you were a pain in the ass.
All that summer at the cottage
watching you, waiting for you
and then that one morning for one moment
turning my back and turning again
to find you face down in the water.

I wouldn't call it love that pulled you
up by the arm and thumped you on the back
so hard your head snapped,
shook you till your face streamed snot
and tears, till you screamed, till you promised
never to tell, till I couldn't see you for the sun
and the sound of my own crying, fist
in the guts that taught me for the first time
how words like that are just a clumsy warning
scrawled at the border of a terrifying country.

Little sister:
most of the time you were just that.
A royal pain in the ass.
When I left for college
you were still playing dressup;
It's only lately we've become
like any women,
starting from scraps of the past
and the rest of our lives
trying to find words that fit.

*

This pause that stretches between us now
is a tight rope, taut wire alive with waiting,
click of your lighter
catch in your breath
as you exhale smoke
begin:

"We're splitting, Carl and I."

*"A lot of things. He   he tried
to beat me up, hit me with his fists
at first, we got a marriage counsellor
but*

       (First, he hit you with his fists.
       First, he hit you.)

*"but   then he   he came at me
with a hammer   tore my shoulder
broke my nose . . .*

*"I've been in one of those houses
you know   for battered women . . .*

*"Pretty good   met some women here
it's alright   I'm okay
now   I . . ."*

Your voice falls away from me
into the lie you couldn't possibly finish
and like the cramped limb that wakes
the sleeper from a nightmare, stab of pain
in my palm, white grip of it
on the telephone receiver, pulls me up
into this room and if you were here, I swear
I could shake you till your head snapped.
Shake you the way a mother will shake a child
who has run beyond her into a scream
of brakes, as if she could shake her
into safety and herself free
of her own fierce helplessness.

*

You are crying now
and the sound reaches for me
through the distances
your husband's hands have forced
between us;
between what we must live
and what we can tell.

I think of all those proverbs
only a woman would use.
Our grandmother's cold comfort;

Marry in haste, repent at leisure.

*You've made your bed. Now you must
lie in it.*

Wisdom of women
whose only choice
was to choose someone else
and a lifetime at the halted limit
of that reaching.
All those dreams of rescue
we dreamed we'd put aside.

Your voice against all that.

Three thousand miles away
in a city I barely know
the man you love
has beaten you with a hammer
and if what needed to be said
were something a woman could make
from whatever she had on hand,
like a cut-down dress
like a good warm coat,
I would stay up all night
to finish it for you.

*

In the house that sheltered you
a woman's hands have rubbed your shoulders,
brought you tea and the names of lawyers,
the titles of books that might help.
And when you couldn't stand it,
when terror was a muffled weight
on your chest, thick as fur
over your mouth,
there was always a woman there
to hold you.

It means you'll survive all this
though we both know you'll never
get over it. There'll always be a need
for something tougher: a skin you could wrap
your heart in, fold it away
from this grieving that stuns you
with its news of a death.

"I only needed to hear your voice," you tell me
"Just for a while. It's better now. Goodnight."

"Goodnight. Take care of yourself."

But sleep comes piecemeal,
teased by the goblin shapes
of what I could have, should have said.
I will be glad for morning,
for the brief light that delivers us
into its own kind of certainty,
where the dream you woke me from
becomes a message I can puzzle over.
Even now, I know
enough about dreams to suspect
that I'm the dog and the children
as well as myself
but it doesn't change anything.
And the love I feel for you
is like the story a mother tells her child
at bedtime, knowing it only serves
to carry her into a land of strangers
where she must dream her own rescue
from whatever scraps and fragments of it
she finds, wrecked there.

THESE THINGS HAPPEN

and the TV news reports
the discovery of a new born
baby whose mother left him
in a Salvation Army used
clothing bin in downtown Detroit

but not how her face
looked empty curve of her
hands as the lid banged shut
sharp metal echo through the
dark streets the city closing
in around her

the reports are indignant
although they wouldn't be if
she'd seen him off to war and he'd
been killed then
we'd see her face
that lost bewildered look
such women have as they
lay flowers on some
monument

these things happen
and the official language
indicates their meanings
although in other words
it comes to the same thing
flesh has its own vocabulary
the dulled eyes and broken
gestures of a woman's hands
that speak of how the life
she makes
can be sloughed off
like an old suit
something that doesn't fit
and nothing ever new
or ever really
her own

COMING THROUGH

It's the time of day you like the best: that hour
just before dark, when the colours
and shapes of things seem to forget
their daylit boundaries, so that the sound
of someone whistling in the street is the last pink
light on the horizon, fading through other sounds
of traffic and laughter into lilac, into blue-grey.

Nothing is solid now. Against the sky the trees
are so still they vibrate with the effort
of holding themselves in and the walls of the houses
hesitate as if they might dissolve,
revealing the lives behind them, intricate
and enchanted as the lives of dolls.

You had a friend who opened
secrets for you like that
and when you think of her now
it's mostly on evenings like this one,
when the last of that light
which is itself a kind of silence
gives to the room a mirror-like quality,
translucent as memory.

You can almost smell the coffee you'd make for her then,
see the steam rising from the blue cup, her fingers
curled around it, warming themselves.
You can still see the way her hands moved
when she talked, creating a second language,
drawing you in
to the very centre of her words
where the real stories lived.
And her eyes, following your sentences
wherever they led,
until it seemed those nights
you entered each others' lives
as if they were countries,
not the superficial ones that maps create,
or ordinary conversation, but the kind

that twist and plummet underneath a day's events
like the labyrinths you followed as a child
or the new-made world that opened
for you alone when you discovered lying.

You lived within each other then
and each of those nights was a place
you inhabited together, a place
you thought you could return to always.

The headlights from a passing car outside
startle the bright ghosts that gather
in the corners of the room. It makes you remember
the bedroom you had as a child
and how you huddled under the covers like a snail,
watching the goblins who lived in the dresser drawers
glide across the mirror and over the ceiling
into your bed. It was the smell of your teddy bear
that saved you then and the satin edge of the blanket
at your cheek as smooth as sleep.
It was the voices of your parents in the kitchen,
far away as growing up and as safe. Even by day
your parents filled their lives
with such a confidence,
you believed they had been born into adulthood
or arrived there, years ago, before
there were any history books or maps, and made it
their very own sort of place. Not like you.
Stubbing your toes on the furniture that changed
overnight, your arms suddenly appearing
from the sleeves of your favourite jacket
like a scarecrow's
like somebody else.

You can laugh at it now, although
it's only lately you've begun to realize
how much of your time you've spent like that:
almost a guest in your own life,
wandering around waiting for someone
or something to explain things to you.

It was always late when she left
and you'd stand in the doorway, waiting
till she'd started the car, then
sit in the dark yourself
for the twenty minutes or so it took her
to drive home. As you locked up, checked the kids
you could imagine her doing the same thing,
so that on those nights sleep was just another opening,
another entry you made together.

She's been dead for a long time now.
You'd thought that would make a difference
but it hasn't. And though you feel angry
at your need for an explanation
it's still there. As if she owed it to you, somehow.
As if somebody did.

Oh, you've learned the accepted wisdom of it.
Can even feel yourself healing these days, almost
strong enough now to re-enter the places
you inhabited together. And you know
you'll never figure it all out anyway;
any more than you can understand your neighbours
from what you see in their lighted windows
framed, like public advertisements.

And yet.

A part of you resists all that.
Resists it with the pure, unthinking stubbornness
you lived in as a child,
that harder wisdom
you are re-discovering now.
Some people are a country
and their deaths displace you.
Everything you shared with them
reminds you of it: part of you in exile
for the rest of your life.

TO GET TO YOU

It's never easy.
Even the effort of a few steps
from the bedroom to the kitchen, say,
or a few muscles, opening my eyes
to find you, still there in bed beside me
is an act of magic or faith,
I'm never sure which.

All I know is that it's learned
by doing, over and over again,
like any other trick,
until you don't need to think about it.
Like now. Like the way I'm walking home
to you through this city I've learned to accept
as the only kind there is: five o'clock,
night coming down and rain
just hard enough
to make the crowds on the corners shove a little
when a bus finally splashes to the stop.
Outside a restaurant, two men shake hands
and a little boy holds his father's
as they watch a toy airplane turning in a shop window.
It could be anywhere. But what I want you to notice
are the women. They are wearing white nurses shoes,
or dirty sneakers or high-heeled boots.
They carry briefcases and flowers, bags of groceries
as they hurry home to husbands and kids,
lovers, ailing parents, friends.
We all have the same look somehow.
See: over there by the bank
how that stout woman lowers her eyes
when she passes that group of boys,
how her movement's mimed
by the blonde, turning her head
when a car slows down beside her.
Even the high-pitched giggle of the girls
in that bunch of teenagers is a signal
I've learned to recognize. Tuned in

by my own tightened muscles, jawline or shoulders.
In fact, you might study the shoulders.
The line of the backbone, too; arms and hips,
the body carried
like something the woman's not sure what to do with.

I've already told you that this is an ordinary city.
There are maps of it and lights to show us
when to walk, where to turn.
What I want you to know is that it isn't enough.

On a trip to Vancouver once
I discovered clearer landmarks. Red ones,   .
sprayed on sidewalks all over the city.
They marked the places
where a woman had been raped,
so that when I stepped out of a coffee shop
to find one on the pavement by the laundromat
geography shifted.
Brought me to the city I'd always imagined
happening in dark alleys, deserted parking lots,
to somebody else. Brought me home in a way,
no longer the victim of rumours or old news,
that red mark planted in the pavement
like the flag of an ancient, immediate war.

I used to hope it was enough
that you were gentle
that I love you,
but what can enough mean, anymore
what can it measure?

How many rapes were enough
for those women in Vancouver
before they got stencils and spray paint
made a word for their rage?
How many more until even that word
lost its meaning
and the enemy was anything that moved out there.
Anything male, that is.

How can any woman say
she loves a man enough
when every city on the planet
is a minefield
she must pick her way through
just to reach him?

It's not that we manage it, though.
It's that we make it look so easy.
These women wearing their fear
like a habit of speech or movement
as if this were the way
the female body's meant to be.
The way I turn the last corner now,
open the door to find you
drinking wine and reading the newspaper,
another glass already filled
and waiting on the coffee table.

When I turn on the hall light
the city will retreat into the rain,
the tiny squares of yellow
marking the other rooms
where men and women greet each other.
It's a matter of a few steps,
magic or faith, though it's not that simple.
The way the rain keeps watering the cities of the world.
How it throws itself against our window,
harder, more insistent,
so that we both hear.

—————————————PADDY WEBB—————————————

*Paddy Webb was born in Essex, England, where she lived until emigrating
to Canada in 1966. She is currently living in Montreal (where she teaches at
McGill University) and in the Eastern Townships of Quebec. Paddy's
poems have appeared in various publications in England, Australia,
U.S.A. and Canada. Her published works are "Between Two Fires",
Delta Canada, 1971; and "Children and Milkweed", Priapus Press,
Berkhamsted, England, 1978. More recently she is writing novels, and
hopes to publish "Like Niobe" next year. A second novel, "On the
Margins" is nearing completion.*

NINE MONTHS

february fallen snow
melts on the hills   and blue jays
hang about the houseside tree
certain   now winter has so
far advanced that they'll be fed
new-tapped warm sap thrusts free
into my cup while the brass bed
rattles
     and your eyes reflect larch-
light   inward flaming willow
clusters of upside-down coal-tits
and squirrel clatter
      in march
moist with syrup-in-ice bits
take me   a sugaring off

august finds me promiscuous
patterned by grass-blades and twigs
picking the nose of my doubt
in a dry season   but big
with promise   belly filled out
since maple juice time
      pockets
of skin moving nervously
under your fingers are me
but not me
     we feel the kick
of tenderness   play name-games
music and meaning
      all tricks
to make the hours pass quickly
as a heaviness weights me

and in a time when sweet pain
cauterizes flesh   singeing
the centre of pleasure
                         doors
in my back open   swinging
on hinges of bone   and through them
a slow wave strains
                        shuddering
like stripping clothes off within my skin

my core explodes   springs
gushes   and nuzzling my thigh is
a small pusing head
                        first snow
falls in soft feathers from wings
beating in secret places
your eyes reflect two faces

GRANDMOTHER

at eighty-three   my grandmother
    smelled baby-fresh damp from the
bath   and oatmeal lavender
    her moist brown eye pecked me
with sudden bright stabbing
    she had a quick ear   also quick
to run with our dog on the sands
    or darn a sock   the needle
flashing and poking at the
    rotten stuff till neat and cleanly
mended

          clean   to my grandmother
    was not a negative virtue
no scrubbed and scoured sterility
    but the scent of rosewood on
opening chests of crisp linen
    knee-warmers   camisoles
and little sachets of dried flowers —
    woodruff   self-heal   agrimony

today   in the cemetery
    I found a bank of wild thyme
to sit and read the gravestones from. . .
    she would have been one hundred
and twelve today. . .
              bruising the fleshy
    aromatic leaves   I thought
of her
      and saw her round the path
    her white hair stark against the yew
dip a can in the tub
               water
    the grave
          and wash the headstone

     clean

BRYONY

bryony I was saying over and over
     bryony   bryony   bryony
I could see the woods   the berries
looped in scarlet strings
     (trip wires for foxes)
I could smell the damp earth-smell
and fungus   moss and fungus
lifting delicate noses
sniffing the steamy air
probing with itchy fingers
the undersides of roots and sinews
     and bleeding
all along the length of their stems

I saw three spindle-trees
     opening warm kernels
     (out of their bursting
     orange sheaths the pistol-
     shots of their exclamations)

abundance   they cried
                spilling
into the winds   the rain
the pungent sweaty air
           falling
on a mulch of leaf-mould
and whispering grasses

in holes left by shrews
and miner-bees
          sifting   sifting
through the choreography
     of branches
          and lifting
     to spatter the clouds

how is the sky ever blue
spotted with such various spores
     I faint to breathe by?

bryony I was saying over and over
     bryony   bryony   bryony

—————————— *LILIANE WELCH* ——————————

Liliane Welch was born in Luxembourg and moved to Sackville, New Brunswick in 1967. Now a Canadian citizen, she studied both in Europe and the U.S. She has published five books of poetry including "Syntax of Ferment", "Brush and Trunks" (Fiddlehead Poetry Books), "Assailing Beats (Borealis Press) and most recently "From the Songs of the Artisans" (Fiddlehead) which focuses, with photos and poems, on the creative process inherent in such crafts as pottery, weaving, engraving, glass making, wood-turning, whittling, surgery. Liliane Welch is also a critic of art and literature. With her husband/philosopher she has written two books of literary criticism on contemporary French poetry: "Emergence: Baudelaire, Mallarme, Rimbaud" (Bald Eagle Press) and "Address: Rimbaud, Mallarme, Butor" (Sono Nis Press). During her sixteen years of teaching at Mount Allison University in Sackville, New Brunswick, she has given con-centrated attention to teaching modern and contemporary French poetry.

HEALERS

ANAESTHETIST: DRIFTING IN ELYSEUM

When he sinks
The butterfly into her vein
Sleep ducks her swiftly
And covets her small breasts.

It kisses their blue stars,
The pentothal and demerol
Seeping further and further
Through limbs and moonstruck face.

He monitors her opaque repose
As the laughing gas
Ponders and gropes
In the lungs, the twilit blood.

She glides over the Styx.
Machine music
Is her consort
As she drifts over Elyseum.

Red her barren womb brims.
She is the absent, vestal
Core of today
Sleeved in hospital greens,

Gathering the mist of poppies,
Each deep, induced breath
Spelling his victory,
Heaving the stone of the dead.

HEALERS

GYNECOLOGIST: ARCHITECT OF FLESH

She can't feel the drive
of the scalpel in the wall
of her flank, the bite
on her naked skin.

It breaks her belly
in scarlet lips,
it cuts the frail domain
of her pain.

He sinks his prongs
into the dark gash,
the opened crock,
the trembling valves and ties.

Within the deep vault
the blood sings
from every vein,
life-sprouts, pulse-shores:

his fingers sense
the knots of a plush cyst,
her womb an urn
to catch

the tears of fear.
Masked Hippocrates,
architect of flesh and
blood, he delivers her

of that tangled growth.
And her dead dreams
he strips of their roots,
stitching the red ridge tight.

HEALERS

ANAESTHETIST: FORDING THE DARK

She lies waiting
veiled in greens,
cut and stitched,
a mound of sleep

under his hand's reach.
A swoop of cocaine
veers and sweeps,
feathers of lark wings

warm her feet.
Atropine nuzzles her
thighs, cold stones
in a drugged grave.

She lies waiting
for his hand's touch,
pale and lost,
dreaming caresses

on a field's mist.
Charting that stream
of oblivion,
the soundless drift,

he crosses Hermes
intent and masked,
briefly robs Hades
and fords the dark.

CALLIGRAPHY OF A MARITIME KITCHEN

In their winter kitchen
a fiddle plays,
on the radio.

Smell of nutmeg, smell
of thyme.
Sunlight,
where her fingers strike
the dough.

Smell of exile, smell
of sage.
In mid-room,
suspended,
the man with
the gleaming face.

FARMER'S WIFE AND C.B.

Voices, company, reach me
from the Trans-Canada.
All afternoon.
Love through the window.
On my C.B., C.B.
My old man I've forgotten.
He drives a tractor.
Hogs. Yapping dogs.
Folded laundry, canned peaches,
cigarette butts, unwashed dishes,
four kids grown mean:
is this my life?

Will I find a lover
from Cape Breton,
with a C.B.?
We'll tear down the highway —
why not right away?
I feed my mother-in-law,
she drools, old sourpuss:
I wish she were dead,
won't show it.
My C.B., my C.B.:
I'm hearing voices,
I'm talking to the world.

ACKNOWLEDGEMENTS

Elizabeth Allen: "Bruises" appeared originally in *Poetry Canada Review*; "Seasons" and "Homestead" appeared originally on CBC Radio *Ambience*; "Preparing for Winter" appeared originally in *NeWest Review*; all reprinted by permission of the author.

Roo Borson: Parts 1, 10, 20 from *Rain*, by Roo Borson, reprinted by permission of John Flood, Penumbra Press, and the author.

Elizabeth Brewster: "Double Inventory" and "Assignment" printed by permission of author. "Displaced Person" from *Sunrise North* by Elizabeth Brewster © 1972 by Clarke Irwin (1983) Inc. Used by permission.

Ronnie Brown: Printed by permission of the author.

Heather Cadsby: Printed by permission of the author.

Lorna Crozier: "Woman From the West Coast" appeared originally in *Poetry Canada Review*; "Stillborn" from *The Weather*, Coteau Books, © 1983 by Lorna Crozier; "Wild Geese" printed by permission of the author; "Pavlova" appeared originally in *Saturday Night*, reprinted by permission of the author.

Fran Davis: Printed by permission of the author.

Mary di Michele: Printed by permission of the author.

Susan Glickman: Printed by permission of the author.

Diana Hayes: "Take Your Heart to the River" appeared originally in *Quarry*, Vol. 32-3; "As Shadows Through These Hundred Trees" and "This is the Moon's Work" appeared originally in the League of Canadian Poets' "lines" series, reprinted by permission of the author.

Maggie Helwig: "The Numbering at Bethlehem" appeared originally in *Ethos*; reprinted by permission of the author.

Pat Jasper: "Imprints" appeared originally in *Origins*; "Intimations" appeared originally in *Fiddlehead*; reprinted by permission of the author.

ACKNOWLEDGEMENTS

Elizabeth Jones: "Daughters" printed by permission of the author; "Thanksgiving at Black Rock", "Two Women", "Lying In", and "Child Dressing" from *Flux*, Borealis, © 1977 by Elizabeth Jones, reprinted by permission of the author.

Diane Keating: "Affirmation", "Mad Apples", "Bottom of the Garden", and "Fecundity" from "No Birds or Flowers", Exile Editions, © 1983, Diane Keating; reprinted by permission of the author.

Joy Kogawa: Printed by permission of the author.

Rosalind MacPhee: "Decoy" from *Scarecrow*, Fiddlehead Poetry Books, © 1979 by Rosalind MacPhee; "Nares Lake" from *What Place is This?*, Coach House Press, © 1983, by Rosalind MacPhee; "Morning" appeared originally in *Canadian Forum*; all reprinted by permission of the author.

Susan McMaster: "The Reading Ends at Nine" appeared originally in *Event*, vol. 12, No. 1; "Three Women Camping", "Anniversary" and "Spring Over Grown" from *Seven Poems, Ouroboros*, © 1983 by Susan McMaster; "Three Women Camping" appeared in *Arc*, 8-9, 1983; "Spring Over Grown" appeared in *Quarry*, 31/4; all reprinted by permission of author.

Sharon Nelson: "A Footstool in Heaven", "Horticulture", and "Farm Report" from *Mad Women & Crazy Ladies*, Sunken Forum Press, © 1983 by Sharon Nelson. "A Footstool in Heaven" appeared in *The Radical Reviewer*; "Farm Report" appeared in *Room of One's Own*; all reprinted by permission of the author.

Janis Rapoport: "Child's Drawing with Crayon" from *Winter Flowers*, Hounslow, © 1979 by Janis Rapoport; all printed by permission of the author.

Charlene Sheard: Printed by permission of the author.

——————————ACKNOWLEDGEMENTS——————————

Carolyn Smart: "Flying" printed by permission of the author; "Outside Grand Forks, North Dakota" from *Swimmers in Oblivion*, York, © 1981, Carolyn Smart; reprinted by permission of the author.

Miriam Waddington: "Night in October" from *The Second Silence*, Ryerson, © 1955 by Miriam Waddington; "The Transplanted" from *The Visitants*, Oxford, © 1981 by Miriam Waddington; "Losing Merrygorounds" and "The Terrarium" from *The Glass Trumpet*, Oxford, © 1966 by Miriam Waddington; "The Wheel" from *The Price of Gold*, Oxford, © 1976 by Miriam Waddington; all reprinted by permission of the author.

Bronwen Wallace: Printed by permission of the author.

Paddy Webb: "nine months" appeared in *Priapus Eighteen*, Berkhamsted, England, Summer 1969; "grandmother" appeared in *Cyan Line*, Vol. 1, No. 1, Fall 1975; these and "bryony" printed by permission of the author.

Liliane Welch: "Healers" from *From the Songs of the Artisans*, Fiddlehead Poetry Books, © 1983 by Liliane Welch; "Farmer's Wife and C.B." from *October Winds*, Fiddlehead Poetry Books, © 1980 by Liliane Welch; "Calligraphy of a Maritime Kitchen" from *Syntax of Ferment*, Fiddlehead Poetry Books, © 1979 by Liliane Welch; all reprinted by permission of the author.